The Winterthur Library Revealed:
Five Centuries of Design and Inspiration

Neville Thompson

with

Bert Denker
E. Richard McKinstry
Lois Olcott Price
Jeanne Solensky

Oak Knoll Press
in association with
Winterthur Museum,
Garden & Library

First Edition, 2003
Published by Oak Knoll Press
310 Delaware Street, New Castle, Delaware, USA
Web http://www.oakknoll.com
and Winterthur Museum, Garden & Library
Winterthur, Delaware 19735
www.winterthur.org

ISBN: 1-58456-110-6 P/B
        1-58456-120-3 H/B
Title: The Winterthur Library Revealed: Five Centuries of Design and Inspiration
Typographer: Spearhead International
Editor: Onie Rollins
Publishing Directors: Susan Randolph & J. Lewis von Hoelle
Photo Credits: Russ Kennedy, iv; all others courtesy Winterthur Library.

This catalogue accompanies an exhibition at

The Grolier Club
December 9, 2003 – February 7, 2004

Winterthur
May 1 – July 24, 2004

Partial funding for the exhibition provided by
the Friends of Winterthur and the Gladys Krieble
Delmas Foundation.

Cover illustrations:
Thomas Sheraton, *The Cabinet-Maker, Upholsterer, and General Artists' Encyclopaedia,*
1804–7 (entry 19).
Belcher Mosaic Glass Company, *Trade Catalogue,*
1886 (entry 97).

This work was printed and bound in China on 100# archival, acid-free paper meeting the require-
ments of the American Standard for Permanence of Paper for Printed Library Materials.

Contents

Winterthur's Italianate staircase with azaleas in full bloom.

Foreword

Winterthur is a unique national treasure. One of the last great American country estates, this former home of the du Pont family comprises some 1,000 acres amid the gentle, rolling hills of Delaware's scenic Brandywine Valley. Our history dates from 1839, when Jacques Antoine and Evelina du Pont Bidermann built the first house on the estate and named the property Winterthur, after Bidermann's ancestral home in Switzerland.

An imposing mansion, a great collection of art and antiques, an outstanding garden, and a thriving agricultural and dairy operation on extensive land holdings—all hallmarks of a country estate—form an important part of Winterthur's past. These jewels in the Winterthur "crown" were brought to their glory in the early 20th century under the watchful eye of Henry Francis du Pont, the last private resident of the estate and the founder, in 1951, of Winterthur Museum.

Du Pont's Winterthur today offers a rare combination of beauty, history, art, and learning. The extraordinary museum collection of early American decorative arts remains without equal. The brilliantly conceived naturalistic garden provides a sense of peace and calm amid a romantic landscape. The nationally renowned library serves as an important center for the study of American art and culture. Together these resources contribute greatly to the fulfillment of our mission to inspire, enlighten, and delight all our visitors.

We take great pride in presenting this volume of outstanding library treasures. They are but a small part of all that is Winterthur. We invite you to visit us soon. Celebrate the best in style and craftsmanship. Be enthralled by the signature beauty. Discover our world set apart.

Leslie Greene Bowman
Director

Preface

In 2001 Winterthur celebrated its 50th anniversary as the foremost center for the enjoyment and study of the decorative arts. In accordance with the wishes of founder Henry Francis du Pont, the mission of the institution has always been one of education. Forming a vital component in the fulfillment of that mission is the Winterthur Library—for too long a little-known treasure that was as important to du Pont as his incomparable collection of decorative arts.

As is revealed in this volume, the Winterthur Library is a gem. From the core holdings supplied by du Pont from his private library to the more than 87,000 volumes and 500,000 manuscripts and images that it encompasses today, this repository founded to further the field of material culture includes resources like no other.

When considering the field of material culture and the role that objects play in the study and history of culture, it is necessary to investigate all stages of the process of creating, marketing, and using an object when attempting to discover what that object can tell us about a particular period in time. Such is the focus of *The Winterthur Library Revealed: Five Centuries of Design and Inspiration*.

From printed furniture patterns of the 16th century to colonial-revival silver design drawings of the 20th, the five centuries of books, drawings, and ephemera seen here represent the work of artisans, manufacturers, advertisers, and countless other hands through which the material surroundings of our everyday lives have passed.

The volume opens with an overview of the pioneering scholarship in the field of material culture and the collectors, including H. F. du Pont, who helped shape the study of household furnishings and their surroundings. We then consider artisans and designers, their drawings, and the source material that inspired them to produce the objects that they did. Next examined is the marketing and advertising that brought an artisan's works to the attention of the consumer. A discussion of the purchases and design choices made by those consumers then follows. Completing the cycle is an in-depth look at the stories of two museum collection objects as told through the numerous and varied resources in the library. Through these case studies—highlighting the ways in which library materials can illuminate any one piece—we succinctly sum up the comprehensive collecting policy that has steadfastly guided the Winterthur Library this past half-century.

Henry Francis du Pont in the garden at Winterthur, ca. 1950. *Winterthur Archives*

Introduction

The Winterthur Library owes its initial shape to one man and one program. The man was Henry Francis du Pont, the last owner of the Winterthur estate and the founder, in 1951, of Winterthur Museum. It was du Pont's private collection of books on American art and antiques and their European background that provided the core deposit for the institution's library. The program in question is the Winterthur Program in Early American Culture (WPEAC). Begun in 1952, fostered by du Pont, and offered in partnership with the University of Delaware, the graduate-degree program provides an unparalleled training ground for curators and other scholars in the field of decorative arts and material culture. Its breadth of focus on American art, history, and literature has required a library equally as comprehensive. It is the Winterthur program, therefore, that has driven collecting well beyond the bounds of what is typical of museum libraries.

In a 1952 letter to Winterthur director Charles Montgomery, Frank Sommer, who presided over the first great expansion of the library, caught this very spirit. After a wildly successful book-buying tour of England, Sommer wrote that he was "wallowing in books, books, books—Adam, Wittkower, Palladio ... [t]he course [WPEAC] next term should be a humdinger if I can do my materials justice." Sommer set the pattern to be followed by two subsequent library directors—a collection policy shaped by the research needs of students and scholars defining the arts, history, and culture of the United States with the boldest of brush strokes. The library would collect architectural pattern books, artisan price and account books, domestic advice manuals, trade catalogues, cookbooks, diaries, travel accounts, fabric swatch books, full runs (with their covers) of the great consumer magazines, dozens of European ornament books—all offering a rare and extraordinary visual catalogue of American history, art, and design.

In 1969 the library moved from the main museum to its present home, the Louise du Pont Crowninshield Research Building. The new accommodations offer separate spaces for the Printed Book and Periodical Collection; the Winterthur Archives, with its collections on both the history of the estate and the museum; the slide library; the Joseph Downs Collection, established in 1955, now encompassing manuscripts, ephemera, and microfilm; and a visual resources section the most important piece of which is the Decorative Arts Photographic Collection, a unique archive of photographs of American objects whose makers are known.

Over the years the library has grown through the generosity of many donors. Since 1963 the Friends of Winterthur has been a major force in shaping the collections. They have given us Nivelon's *Rudiments of Genteel Behavior* (London, 1737); the magnificent French peddler's trade catalogue (Paris, 1806–13); the Norwich worsted pattern book (Norwich, Eng., 1794–97); James Barron's *Modern and Elegant Designs* ... (London, 1814), and numerous others. Among the members of the Friends, none has been more generous than Edmond L. Lincoln. A great collector in his own right, Ed Lincoln has brought to the library not only generosity but also a deep discernment about the library's needs. To him we owe the Gillow & Co. drawing of chairs; several Pillement ornament plates; a rare and beautiful copy of Gaetano Landi, *Architectural Decorations* (London, 1810)—with help from the Friends—and André-Charles Boulle's *Nouveaux deisseins de meubles* ... (Paris,

17–), to name but a few. Ed Lincoln has been the most important individual donor to the library since H. F. du Pont himself.

In addition to single volumes, the Winterthur Library has been the beneficiary of large and important gifts: the Waldron Phoenix Belknap, Jr. Collection of American Art; the Edward Deming Andrews Memorial Shaker Collection, one of

The WPEAC class of 1954 in the Memorial Library, the former du Pont family library at Winterthur.

the three leading Shaker collections in the country; and the Maxine Waldron Collection of Children's Books and Paper Toys. Library materials now encompass more than 500,000 items.

Open to all, the library supports the work of students, scholars, collectors, and the interested general public. Many donors have created scholarship and fellowship endowments that allow Winterthur to offer financial support, on a competitive basis, to researchers from around the globe, facilitating their use of all the institution's collections. The library has received the support and recognition of Lois and Henry McNeil, the National Endowment for the Humanities, the Andrew W. Mellon Foundation, the Henry Luce Foundation, and the Barra Foundation, among others. It is a member of the Independent Research Libraries Association, the Research Libraries Group, the Philadelphia Area Consortium of Special Collections Libraries, the McNeil Center for Early American Culture, and the Association of Research Institutes in Art History.

This magnificent catalogue, produced in company with a Grolier Club exhibition, stands as a testament to one of the splendid jewels in Winterthur's "crown." We hope that it inspires further interest in the library, attracts new scholars

A view of the Winterthur Galleries and main museum buildings, with the Louise du Pont Crowninshield Research Building in the right foreground, ca. 1997.

and donors, and encourages a renewed appreciation of Henry Francis du Pont's Winterthur—a great American country estate.

Gary Kulik
Deputy Director for Library, Collections
Management, and Academic Programs
Waldron Phoenix Belknap Librarian

2. Wallace Nutting. *Ready for the Afternoon*, 1912–17. Hand-colored platinum print.

Chapter 1

Shaping the Field: Early Collecting and Scholarship

by Lois Olcott Price

By the last decades of the 19th century, a sweeping nostalgia and desire to connect specific objects with historic personages prompted an interest in the history of American decorative arts. The "colonial" kitchen on display at the 1876 Centennial International Exhibition in Philadelphia proved to be a major attraction, and objects that were associated with the Pilgrims, George Washington, or any colonial dignitary became venerated relics. In 1909, as part of the Hudson-Fulton Celebration, the Metropolitan Museum of Art mounted an exhibition that brought together a significant collection of American antiques in a public venue for the first time. As the colonial-revival movement spread to the broader public, every man wanted a piece of history, and books on collecting and furnishing homes with antiques proliferated. Imagemakers such as Wallace Nutting populated interiors with costumed figures that fueled the public's yearning for a simpler life symbolized by colonial furnishings.

At the same time, a scholarly approach to American decorative arts and an appreciation of their aesthetic as well as historic value was growing among serious collectors. Early proponents such as Irving Whitall Lyon (1891), Esther Singleton (1901), and Francis Bigelow (1906) introduced the use of documentary evidence, including inventories and advertisements, to illustrate the activities of early craftsmen. With the opening of the American Wing of the Metropolitan Museum of Art in 1924 and the 1929 Girl Scouts Loan Exhibition in New York, American domestic furnishings were presented as art objects in a chronological, regional, and historical context. These exhibits provided the impetus for collectors who sought information almost as avidly as objects. The movement to document, research, and publish scholarly information about American decorative arts had taken root, and H. F. du Pont would soon found the library that played a significant role in shaping the field.

Although it grew out of a personal and family collection, the Winterthur Library was, from the beginning, conceived as a tool for educating graduate students and providing the resources necessary for advanced scholarship in the decorative arts. Well before 1946 du Pont had begun buying material in anticipation of the library's needs. Fortunately, his perspective was both deep and broad. His purchases laid the foundation for important scholarly advances as well as developments in the field of material culture. We all are beneficiaries of his foresight.

1.   Esther Singleton, *The Furniture of Our Forefathers*. New York: Doubleday, Page, and Company, 1901. Deluxe edition printed on Imperial Japan paper, no. 34 of 50, with critical description of plates by Russell Sturgis. Hand-colored photogravure.

NK2406 S61a* pt. 2 Printed Book and Periodical Collection, gift of Mrs. James H. Dawson

Ranked with Irving Whitall Lyon and Luke Vincent Lockwood, Esther Singleton was part of the first generation of authors to use historical documents such as estate inventories, newspaper advertisements, and cabinetmakers' price books to date and categorize American antiques. She sought to place antiques within an accurate social and cultural context that renounced most of the fanciful illusions current at the time. Singleton served as editor of the *Antiquarian* (1923–30) and was author of numerous texts. The frontispiece seen here illustrates Washington's bedroom at Mount Vernon, with a note that all the furniture is original. Although a revered figure is cited, the emphasis here and in the text is on documentation and authenticity.

1.

2.	Wallace Nutting, *Ready for the Afternoon,* 1912–17. Hand-colored platinum print. *(Photo, facing page 1)*

02x63 Downs Collection

Wallace Nutting was an early collector and promoter of American decorative arts. His publications, furniture reproductions, and widely advertised and readily available photographs of colonial-revival scenes fueled nostalgia and an interest in American history and art. Much of his work carries an implicit message promoting a return to the earlier values of home, hearth, and family. This photograph of the front hall of the Wentworth-Gardner house (1760) in Portsmouth, New Hampshire, shows one of several historic houses Nutting owned and charged admission to tour. Nutting numbered each of his images; this example is E, G 9035. The letters refer to sizes in which the image was available: E = 11×14 inches at a cost of \$5; G = 16×20 inches at a cost of \$8.

3.

3.	Mary H. Northend, *Colonial Homes and Their Furnishings.* Boston: Little, Brown, and Company, 1912.

NA707 N87 c. 2 Printed Book and Periodical Collection, bequest of Miss Katrina Kipper

Mary Harrod Northend was a native of Salem, Massachusetts, whose books and photographs helped popularize the collecting of American decorative arts. Focusing on the charm of colonial furnishings in domestic settings, her books project a romantic rather than scholarly view, where a tasteful colonial appearance is more important than authenticity. Northend amassed an unsurpassed collection of photographs of private collections and interiors, which she and other authors used repeatedly. Those photographs—some 2,200 prints made from the original glass-plate negatives—now reside in the Winterthur Library.

4.	Eliza Calvert Hall, *A Book of Hand-Woven Coverlets.* Boston: Little, Brown, and Company, 1912.

NK9112 H17 Printed Book and Periodical Collection

Eliza Calvert Hall Obenchain was born and resided in Bowling Green, Kentucky, where she was best known for her poems, stories, and essays about Kentucky life that were published in periodicals such as *Scribner's* and *Cosmopolitan. A Book of Hand-Woven Coverlets* explores the charm and history of coverlets through folklore and oral interviews, an approach that emphasizes the memoirs of women and is consistent with Hall's active involvement in the suffrage movement.

4.

5. Robert and Elizabeth Shackleton, *Quest of the Colonial.* 1907; reprint, New York: Century Company, 1921.

NK2406 S52 Printed Book and Periodical Collection

Beginning with a few chance purchases, Robert and Elizabeth Shackleton developed a taste for antiques, used them to furnish their home, and continued to write about their quest for several decades. Robert began his law and collecting careers in Ohio. By 1895 he had become associate editor of the *Saturday Evening Post* and moved to Connecticut.

With authors such as Mary Harrod Northend, the Shackletons brought collecting to the attention of the American public. However, they eschewed established dealers. Because they valued the personal histories that often accompanied objects found in less-commercial settings, the Shackletons pursued antiquing as a pastime that justified pleasant journeys to quaint locales.

6. Francis Hill Bigelow, *Historic Silver of the Colonies and Its Makers.* 1917; reprint, New York: Macmillan, 1925.

NK 7112 B59 c. 3 Printed Book and Periodical Collection, gift of Stanley B. Ineson

Francis Hill Bigelow was a scholar, collector, and dealer in American decorative arts with a particular interest in silver. His organization of the 1906 and 1911 exhibits of American silver at the Museum of Fine Arts, Boston, lent the work of colonial artisans a credibility and visibility that had previously been reserved for European silver. Bigelow's *Historic Silver of the Colonies and Its Makers*, which includes photographs of objects from numerous public and private collections, was the first comprehensive survey of American silver. Bigelow was a charter member of the Walpole Society. He relentlessly sought silver from church and private sources, which he then sold to enthusiasts such as Francis Garvan and Judge A. T. Clearwater, whose collections formed the foundation of those at Yale and the Metropolitan Museum of Art.

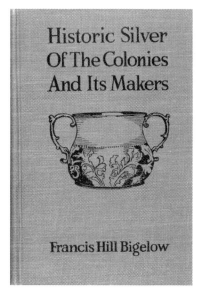

6.

7. R. T. H. Halsey and Elizabeth Tower, *The Homes of Our Ancestors as Shown in the American Wing of the Metropolitan Museum of Art.* Garden City, N.Y.: Doubleday, Page and Company, 1925.

N611 A51h Printed Book and Periodical Collection

Richard Townley Haines Halsey began his collecting career in the 1890s while a member of the New York Stock Exchange. He joined the Grolier Club in 1900 and became a Trustee of the Metropolitan Museum of Art in 1914. His absorption in the study of American antiques led to his resignation from the Stock

Exchange, allowing him to devote his energies to assembling the architectural interiors and collections that became the American Wing at the Met. The opening of that wing in 1924 created a sensation by exhibiting American antiques as both art and cultural documents in chronologically arranged period settings. Incorporating a scholarly reliance on original documents, *The Homes of Our Ancestors* interprets early American life and virtues through those furnishings. Halsey, his wife, Elizabeth Tower, and others of his generation saw promotion of the tasteful simplicity of high-quality antiques as the key to preserving what was unique in the American character amid a flood of cultural change.

8.   Girls Scouts Loan Exhibition, New York, 1929. Silver gelatin print.

75HF.1 P112 ovz Winterthur Archives

On September 25, 1929, a groundbreaking exhibition opened at the American Art Association Galleries on Madison Avenue and 57th Street, New York. The organizers and lenders included the most prominent collectors and scholars of

8.

the period who placed a premium on objects that met high standards for beauty, craftsmanship, and design. Although some choices still reflected an earlier antiquarian approach and one that associated objects with historic figures, this exhibit marked the acceptance of American decorative arts as aesthetic objects. As the largest lender, H. F. du Pont was heavily involved in the arrangement of the exhibition in roomlike settings. The federal-style New York sideboard and dining and pier tables that dominate the installation seen here now reside at Winterthur. The abundance of floral arrangements with a single type of bloom is typical of du Pont's design aesthetic.

9. William MacPherson Hornor Jr., *Blue Book, Philadelphia Furniture: William Penn to George Washington*. Philadelphia: By the author, 1935.

    RRNK2438 P54h Printed Book and Periodical Collection, gift of Henry Francis du Pont

William Hornor was a well-connected Philadelphian with access to the major private collections in the area. He exploited that access to research and write the first scholarly book on American furniture that recognized and defined a regional style. Hornor relied on inventories, account books, tax lists, and invoices to chronicle the activities of Philadelphia cabinetmakers and their patrons. His *Blue Book* remains an essential source for anyone studying Philadelphia furniture.

10. H. F. du Pont book purchases from American dealers, 1926–52. Typescript.

    Winterthur Archives

This document systematically records some of the American purchases made by H. F. du Pont during the formative years of the library and the Winterthur Program in Early American Culture. The scope of his purchases, ranging from city directories to manuals on dyeing fabric to design books, established the foundation of the Winterthur Library's collection policy. The following entries illustrate a few of the highlights.

11.

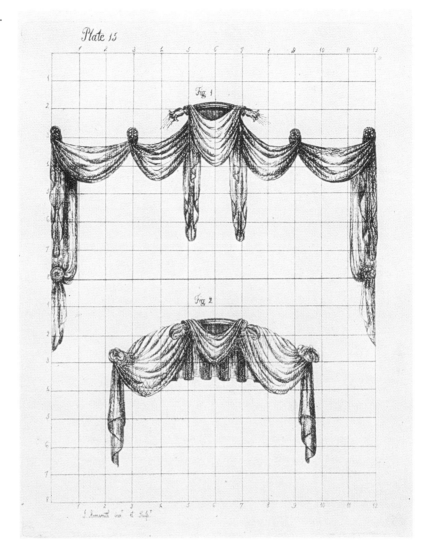

11.   James Arrowsmith, *An Analysis of Drapery; or, The Upholsterer's Assistant*. London: Printed by M. Bell, 1819. Etching.

TT390 A77 Printed Book and Periodical Collection, gift of Henry Francis du Pont

James Arrowsmith was an English upholsterer at a time when the extensive use of fabric for decorating was becoming more common. In the 18th and early 19th centuries, upholsterers were responsible for hanging walls, windows, and beds with fabric as well as applying it to furniture. Keyed to his scale drawings, Arrowsmith provided tables for determining yardage and advice on the design and finishing of decorative hardware that supported the drapes. The plate seen here illustrates a design that extends over two windows and a pier with a cornice in gold or black with gold ends *(top)* and a drapery suitable for a bed *(bottom)*.

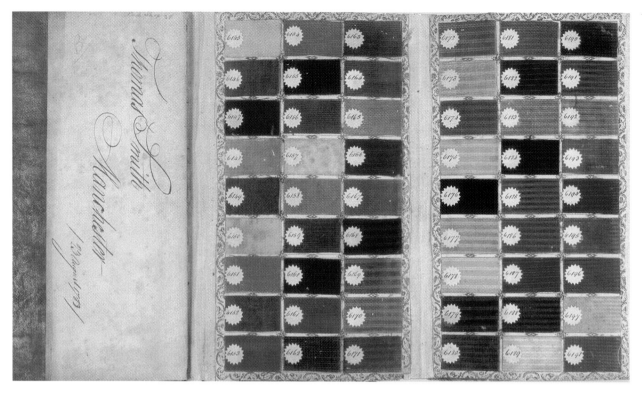

12.   Textile sample book. Inscribed "Thomas Smith,
       Manchester, 23 August 1783." Cotton textiles in leather
       case.

65x698 Downs Collection, gift of Henry Francis du Pont

This sample book of 432 numbered textile swatches is typical of those produced in Manchester, England, in the late 18th century, when the city was the center of cotton cloth production. This volume contains examples of corduroy and cotton velvet—fabrics commonly known as Manchester cloth. The secret of their manufacture was jealously guarded, and these fabrics formed the largest class of exports during the latter part of the 1700s. Frequently used for men's breeches and waistcoats, the fabrics had a sheen similar to that of silk. Pattern books facilitated orders from merchants and retailers and took over the role once played by independent peddlers who traveled with bolts of cloth they hoped were appropriate to their market. Sample books also were used to introduce new patterns and weaves to potential buyers.

13.

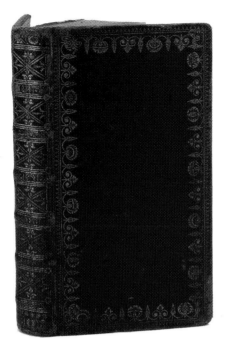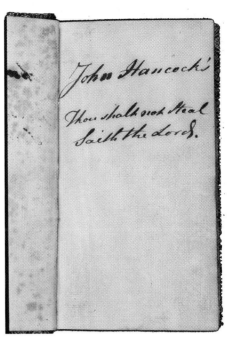

13.   N. Brady D.D. and N. Tate Esq., *A New Version of the Psalms of David Fitted to the Tunes Used in Churches*. Boston: Printed by J. Kneeland and S. Adams in Milk-Street for Wharton and Bowes in Corn-hill, 1765. Fly leaf signed by John Hancock.

M2116 B58 S Printed Book and Periodical Collection, gift of Henry Francis du Pont

Kneeland and Adams printed this book for several different Scottish-immigrant booksellers/binders in Boston. The black morocco binding with raised bands, embroidered endbands, and waxed marbled end papers are consistent with Scottish binding practices of the period. The tooling of the cover and the use of the St. Andrew's cross with the thistle and fleur-de-lis on the spine is also characteristic. Highly ornamented, pre-Revolutionary American bindings are extremely rare. This particularly fine example belonged to John Hancock, whose signature adorns the fly leaf.

14.   Thomas Hope, *Household Furniture and Interior Decoration.*
       London: Longman, Hurst, Beers & Orme, 1807. Etching.

   NK2135 H79 F Printed Book and Periodical Collection, gift
   of Henry Francis du Pont

Thomas Hope spent eight years as a young man traveling and sketching architectural remains in Egypt, Greece, and the eastern Mediterranean. Upon his return
to England he furnished his London mansion in the classical taste, with much of
the furniture made to his design as part of an overall decorating scheme. Hope
published this volume in 1807, documenting and describing each of the major
rooms as well as individual pieces of furniture. The color scheme for the plate
seen here was described as "very vivid" with sky blue walls, crimson sofas, and a
ceiling of pale yellow with azure and sea green. Hope's work was highly influential in introducing the Greek revival and other more exotic classical styles.

15.   Spode book of chinaware shapes and dimensions. Stoke-
       on-Trent, England, ca. 1820. Iron gall and india ink.

   65x574 Downs Collection, gift of Henry Francis du Pont

Founded in 1770, Josiah Spode's pottery in Stoke-on-Trent became a leading
producer of fine china and ceramics. The pottery made earthenware until 1794,
when Spode perfected his formula for bone china. The rapid growth of the business, the proliferation of designs, and the opening of a London warehouse and

15.

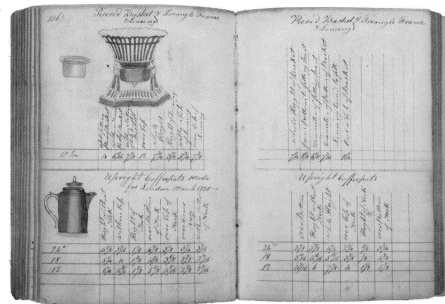

shop necessitated a reliable system for identifying patterns and shapes. This book of shapes, composed for internal use in 1820, fulfilled that need. The dimensions on the left page provide the measurements to which the thrower worked; those on the right supply the final pre-firing dimensions. This volume was probably produced for Spode's London warehouse and shop.

16.   Samuel Ensminger, schoolmaster's book of Pennsylvania German Fraktur letters, 'A' leaf dated August 20, 1821.
Iron gall ink and watercolor.

65x584 Downs Collection, gift of Henry Francis du Pont

In Pennsylvania German schools, instruction in fine handwriting was an important part of the curriculum. Children learned by example, often from Fraktur and other samples produced by the schoolmaster. Although schoolmasters were highly respected in the community, they received low wages, and many turned to Fraktur production as a means of augmenting their income. Samuel Ensminger and his family were among the early settlers of Lancaster County.

16.

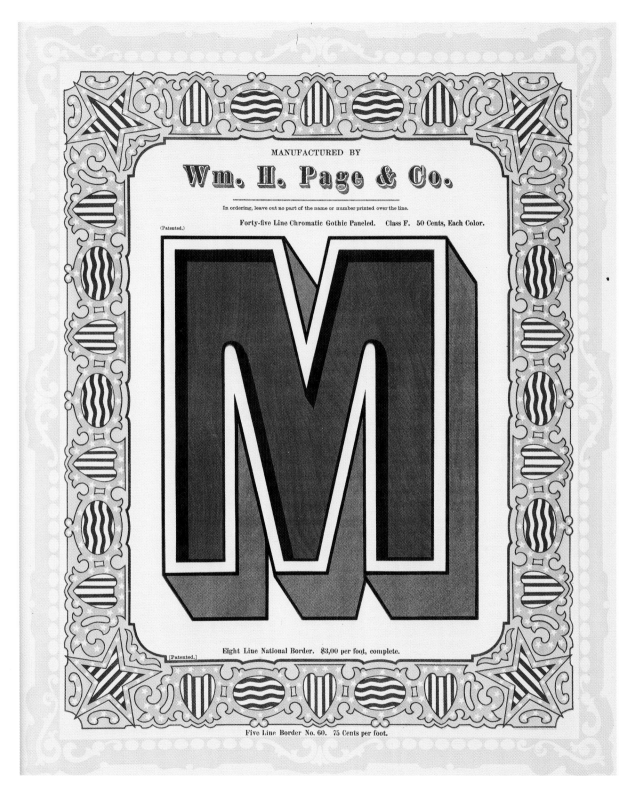

33. Wm. H. Page & Co., *Specimens of Chromatic Wood Type Borders,* & c., 1874. Color-printed plate.

Chapter 2

Shaping the Object: Designers and Makers
by Bert Denker

Original materials—drawings, craft manuals, and design volumes—play a primary role in documenting the work of designers as well as the artisans who actually produced decorative arts objects. A close look at those documents from the past five centuries illustrates the importance of shop tradition as well as innovation in handmade and machine-made goods, providing us with a window to the past and a better understanding of what served as sources of inspiration for both artisans and designers.

Design has always been inextricable from the process of crafting an object. Traditionally, an apprentice was expected not only to learn mechanical skills but also to apply creativity in the fashioning and decoration of an object. In fact, the word *designer* was not recorded and recognized as a distinct occupation until 1662. Earlier than that, artisans produced ornamental designs simply as an adjunct to their main activities.

With the introduction of the design profession, designers played an increasingly crucial role in the evolution of form. It was the publication of the work of those such as Frenchman André-Charles Boulle in the late 17th and early 18th centuries that was responsible for the dissemination of styles beyond national borders. In England the profession of designer was sparked by the establishment of the Government Schools of Design in 1836. And the 1851 Crystal Palace Exhibition in London provided a dual opportunity for craftsmen to display their most recent work and designers to study an international panoply for inspiration.

Despite the proliferation of the profession, many craftsmen continued to design their own work, following established shop traditions. For those artisans, innovation in the production of an object was as important as its design. Of course, technological advances throughout the 19th and 20th centuries had a significant impact on most industries and their craftsmen, leading to the introduction of industrial design as a profession and forcing those designers to be sensitive to the capabilities of new machinery as well as to the market's acceptance or rejection of new styles. The process had indeed evolved.

Over the years, objects produced by artisans and designers have had an incalculable effect on our everyday lives. They tell us much about who we are and what we value. The facts surrounding the creation of those objects—from sources of inspiration to actual production—are nowhere better illustrated and studied than through original materials.

17.   André-Charles Boulle, *Nouveaux Deisseins de Meubles et Ouvrages de Bronze et de Marqueterie.* Paris: Chez Mariette, 17–. Engraving.

NK2550 B76n F Printed Book and Periodical Collection, gift of Edmond L. Lincoln

André-Charles Boulle was born in Paris, the son of a Flemish cabinetmaker. By 1672 he had been appointed Ébéniste du Roi by Louis XIV and installed in lodgings and workshops in the Louvre. Boulle's work in the baroque style employed elaborate marquetry designs in exotic woods and inlay patterns of brass and tortoiseshell. The technique originated in 16th-century Italy and was introduced by Italian craftsmen to France. Boulle is also remembered for his parquet floors and wall panels at Versailles. This folio contains engraved designs for both furniture and bronzes.

18.

18.   *Magazzino di Mobilia.* Florence, Italy: F. Buonaiuti, 1796–97. Hand-colored engraving.

NK2560 M18* Printed Book and Periodical Collection, gift of the Friends of Winterthur

An extremely rare furniture periodical, the *Magazzino di Mobilia* was also extremely short-lived. Only seven numbers were completed. This issue of October 1796, the first, features five engraved plates with exquisite hand coloring and lengthy descriptions of the furniture, architectural details, and metalwares that are illustrated. The text accompanying this plate describes no. 6 as "in English style," no. 5 as a "Roman style side table," and no. 4 as "in the Etruscan style." The Winterthur Library's set of the *Magazzino* is the only one recorded.

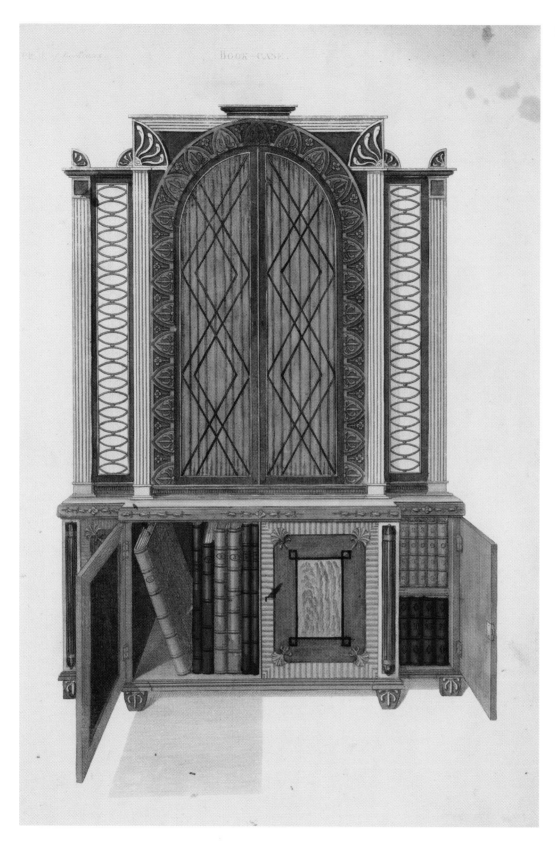

19.   Thomas Sheraton, *The Cabinet-Maker, Upholsterer, and General Artists' Encyclopaedia*. London: By the author, 1804–7. Hand-colored engraving.

NK 2542 S55e F Printed Book and Periodical Collection, gift of the Friends of Winterthur

It would be most difficult to overestimate the influence of English cabinetmaker and furniture designer Thomas Sheraton. His *Cabinet-Maker, Upholsterer, and General Artists' Encyclopaedia* was published immediately before his death. Only 30 parts of the projected 125 were completed. Reflected in this work from his later life are influences from the Egyptian and classical revivals. Only a few copies of the *Encyclopaedia* received the brilliant hand coloring of the engraved plates, as seen here in this "BOOK–CASE," published August 11, 1806.

20.   Joseph Ball & Co., ceramics pattern book. Longton, England, 1857. Ink and watercolor.

83x102 Downs Collection, gift of the Friends of Winterthur

This pattern book for the decoration of ceramics, dated 1857, contains 197 pages of ink-and-watercolor designs as well as many with transfer-printed outlines and hand coloring. It is a compilation of pages that were originally contained in three separate volumes dating from the 1820s to 1840s. The pages show a number of pitchers decorated in the "Gaudy" or Imari style. The volume also includes manuscript formulas for "Ironstone Body," "China Bodies," "Stone China," and lead-based glazes and is identified as belonging to a Joseph Ball, Adderley Green, near Longton, England.

20.

21.   Johann Ferdinand Schreiber, *30 Werkstätten von Handwerkern: Hebst Ihren Hauptlächlichsten werkzeugen und Fabrikaten.* Esslingen am Neckar, Germany: By the author, 18–. Hand-colored engraving.

T45 S37 F Printed Book and Periodical Collection, gift of the Friends of Winterthur

Infinitely valuable for the illustrated documentation of 19th-century craftsmen's shops, *30 Werkstätten* contains detailed, hand-colored engravings. This plate, *Zinngiesser,* shows the interior of a pewterer's workshop. The decorative border of pewtermaking tools and products is equally instructive. Other plates in the volume portray the shops of shoemakers, a bookbinder, cabinetmaker, potter, and blacksmith.

22.

22.   Christian M. Nestell, painted furniture drawing book. New York, 1811–12. Graphite and watercolor.

84x89 Downs Collection, gift of the Friends of Winterthur

This student's drawing book—belonging to 18-year-old Christian Michael Nestell of New York City—is a unique record of the education of an ornamental painter in the United States. The 80 pencil-and-watercolor designs of the unidentified instructor and young Nestell were intended as models for furniture and other decorative arts painted surfaces. The book served Nestell well when he established his shop in Providence, Rhode Island, in 1820, selling Windsor chairs and engaging in "ornamental painting and gilding." This illustration is a design for a painted chair.

23.   Augustus Charles Pugin, *Modern Furniture*. London: M. A. Nattali, 1823. Hand-colored engraving. *(Photo, page 20)*

NK2542 P97m Printed Book and Periodical Collection, gift of the Friends of Winterthur

Augustus Charles Pugin, architect and designer, was a leading advocate for the Gothic style in England. He produced furniture designs for Rudolph Ackermann's *Repository of Arts & c.*, 44 of which were published in 1823 as this volume, *Modern Furniture*. Among the several beds included in this rare compilation is "An English Bed," accompanied by Pugin's description: "THIS design is remarkable for the tasteful simplicity that pervades it. The abandonment of that profusion of drapery which has long been fashionable, has admitted this more chastened style in point of forms, and has long been neglected."

23.

24. Enoch Wood & Sons, *Port of Tarentum,* Burslem, Staffordshire, England, ca. 1830. Engraving.

71x166.8 Downs Collection, gift of the Friends of Winterthur

One of the most common methods of decorating pottery wares in England after the mid-18th century was through the application of transfer-printed designs from thin tissue paper. Intended to decorate a platter in the Enoch Wood & Sons general series of patterns known as "Italian Scenery," *Port of Tarentum* was part of a collection owned by English designer and engraver William Gallimore. Gallimore, who worked for several Staffordshire potters, died in Trenton, New Jersey, at the home of his son. This group of transfer prints and proof prints was acquired from the son by Philadelphia ceramics scholar Edwin AtLee Barber before its purchase by Winterthur Library.

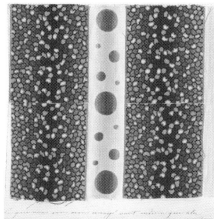

25. *Book of Prices of the United Society of Journeymen Cabinet Makers of Cincinnati, for the Manufacture of Cabinet Ware.* Cincinnati, 1836. Engraved plate.

NK2407 C57 Printed Book and Periodical Collection, gift of the Friends of Winterthur

Price books for cabinetmakers were published in Britain and the United States, and Winterthur Library is fortunate to own exceptional examples. This volume, produced in 1836 for the United Society of Journeymen Cabinet Makers of Cincinnati, Ohio, contains descriptions of bureaus, chairs, an "Egyptian Sideboard," wardrobes, bookcases, bedsteads, and tables, along with the suggested prices in all manifestations of detail.

26. Woven textiles pattern book. France, 1840–46. Gouache and woven textiles.

72x35.1, .27 Downs Collection, gift of the Friends of Winterthur

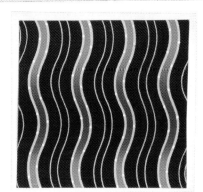

Pattern books for woven textile manufacturers in the 1800s are rare survivals, as are the textiles themselves. The illustrations here are from a book of 210 gouache pattern drawings created for an unidentified French firm. They date from the early 1840s, when France and England were the world centers for the production of fine woven and printed textiles. The volume bears a stationer's label for P. Le Testu Pouen. As seen in these examples, bright colors and strong geometric designs predominate. The pattern on the top, a gouache and printed-and-woven textile, carries the manuscript notation, "Ce que nous vous avons arrangé vaut mieux que cela"—"What we have put in order for you goes better like this."

26.

27.   Paper dolls and clothes, United States, 1850s–80s. Graphite and ink, printed papers.

73x319.47 Maxine Waldron Collection of Children's Books and Paper Toys, gift of Maxine Waldron

Paper dolls and the clothing made for them date from the mid-17th century in Germany. Before 1840 the dolls were printed from engraved plates; later they were lithographed. Both types were hand colored. The first examples published in a periodical appeared in the United States in *Godey's Ladies' Book* for 1859. The selection seen here is unusual for being early examples of homemade creations. The two dolls at the top were copied from *Paper Dolls and How to Make Them: A Book for Little Girls* (New York: A. D. F. Randolph, 1856). In the bottom row, the dolls and their clothes were cut by a thrifty and imaginative child from marbled book papers and a printed advertisement.

28.   *Inventory of the Personal Estate of Michael Allison, deceased,* New York, April 17, 1855.

54x37x28 Downs Collection, gift of the Friends of Winterthur

Michael Allison Sr. was one of New York City's most prominent and successful cabinetmakers in the first half of the 19th century. His furniture in the federal style exhibits a richness of materials, with mahogany veneers and superb craftsmanship. An inventory prepared after Allison's death reveals that his estate was valued at the considerable sum of $27,860.55, confirming his prominence as a businessman.

29.   Thomas Dimmock & Co., ceramics pattern book. Hanley, Staffordshire, England, ca. 1857. Ink and watercolor.

72x307 Downs Collection, gift of the Friends of Winterthur

The firm Thomas Dimmock & Co., and later John Dimmock & Co., flourished throughout the 19th century producing earthenware table- and toiletwares. In 1842 the firm operated two factories in Hanley, Staffordshire, England, and a gilding and decorating workshop in Shelton. This volume contains 147 watercolor and transfer-printed pattern designs for plates and hollowware, including decoration for pink lustre, chinoiserie, "Gaudy Dutch," and "Gaudy Welch." The designs seen here are for the company's neoclassical "Portland" shape.

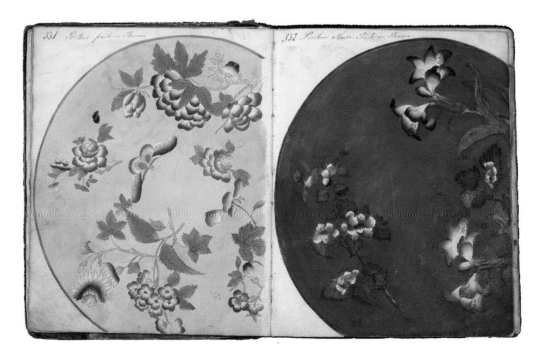

29.

30.   Frederick Crace-Calvert, *Lectures on Coal Tar Colours*.
        Philadelphia: H. C. Baird, 1863.

        *TP893 C88a Printed Book and Periodical Collection, gift of the Friends of
        Winterthur*

English chemist Frederick Crace-Calvert specialized in industrial chemistry, especially that pertaining to the manufacture of coal tar products. This second edition of his *Lectures on Coal Tar Colours* discusses "recent" improvements and progress in dyeing and calico printing since the 1851 Crystal Palace Exhibition in London. Three "lectures" on dyeing materials, colors derived from coal tar, and calico printing are illustrated with numerous fabric samples.

31.   Tattoo design book. Eastern United States, ca. 1865.
        Graphite and colored pencil.

        88x120 Downs Collection, gift of the Friends of Winterthur

Tattoos as body artwork have been in existence since 2000 B.C. Many civilizations have practiced the craft. In the 18th century, English Captain James Cook and his sailors encountered tattooed Polynesian natives and acquired tattoos of their own, beginning a close association in the West of sailors and tattooing. As early as 1840, Herman Melville reported getting tattoos of palm trees, ladies, and lions. This volume of shellacked, naively hand-drawn pencil designs features sentimental and patriotic tattoo patterns with many American images: eagles, ships flying the flag, shields, "Free Trade," and "HOPE."

32.   Owen Jones, *Examples of Chinese Ornament*. London: S. & T.
        Gilbert, 1867. Chromolithographed plate.

        NK1483 J78 Printed Book and Periodical Collection, gift of the Friends of
        Winterthur*

British architect and designer Owen Jones wrote several enormously influential books of ornamental decoration based on designs from pre-history, Islamic, and Asian sources. *Examples of Chinese Ornament* provided decorators and designers with 100 chromolithographed designs taken from porcelain and cloisonné enameled metal objects in the South Kensington Museum (now the Victoria & Albert Museum) and private collections.

33.   Wm. H. Page & Co., *Specimens of Chromatic Wood Type Borders, &c.* Greeneville, Conn.: By the company, 1874. Plate color-printed from wooden type and ornaments. *(Photo, page 12)*

Z250 P13 F Printed Book and Periodical Collection, gift of the Friends of Winterthur

No manufacturer's trade catalogue of the 19th century is more sumptuous than this volume from William H. Page & Co. Issued by the company, which manufactured "seven-eights of all the wood type made," the 98 pages contain elaborate letters and borders arranged in imaginative combinations. The example shown here features the "Eight Line National Border." Other pages illustrate combinations of words such as "SIN," "HUE," "BEAUTIFUL," and "ROSE."

34.   Charles Volkmar, *Trout*, Menlo Park, N.J., ca. 1894. Ink on artist's board.

89x1.9 Downs Collection, gift of the Friends of Winterthur

Born in Baltimore to a family of prominent artists, Charles Volkmar studied there and in France, where he mastered the underglaze ceramic decoration technique popularized and exhibited at the 1876 Centennial International Exhibition in Philadelphia by French manufacturer Haviland & Co. Volkmar returned to the United States in 1879 and established potteries at various locations in the Mid-Atlantic region. He published original designs for china painters in the popular periodical *Art Amateur*. *Trout* was one of the designs for a large fish service. Volkmar was a member of the Salmagundi Club, an artists' association in New York, and he produced and fired the mugs decorated by the members to raise money for the group's library.

35.

35.   Charles Osborne, design for silver spoon, New York, 1904. Ink and gouache on paper.

91x23.139 Downs Collection, gift of the Friends of Winterthur

British-born Charles Osborne's long career as a designer of silver tablewares began at the Whiting Manufacturing Co., New York City, in 1871. From 1878 he worked at Tiffany & Co. as a freelance designer and learned from Edward C. Moore, Tiffany's chief designer who had won a gold medal for the firm's display of Japanesque silver at the 1878 Exposition Universelle in Paris. By 1888 Osborne had returned to Whiting and remained there for the balance of his career (until 1915) as head of design, superintendent, and vice president. Numerous Osborne designs, primarily for silver flatware, are in the Winterthur Library, including those for the souvenir spoons "Old Faithful-Yellowstone," "New Amsterdam," and the "World's Columbian Exposition." Among the ink-and-gouache drawings for flatware are the 1904 "Rose," "Louis XIV," and "Roses" (seen here).

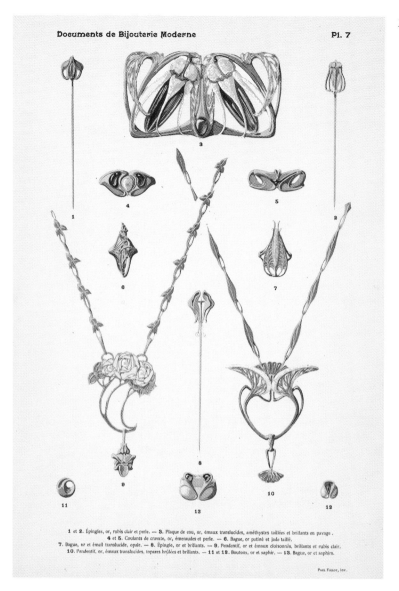

36.   Paul Follot, *Documents de Bijouterie et Orfèvrerie Modernes*. Paris:
        Henri Laurens, 1905. Hand-colored lithograph.

*NK7349 F66 F Printed Book and Periodical Collection, gift of the Friends of
Winterthur*

Parisian artist and sculptor Paul Follot was the son of a prominent wallpaper
manufacturer. He studied under Eugène Grasset at the École Normale
d'Enseignement du Dessin and later designed jewelry and silverware for Julius
Meier-Graefe's shop, La Maison Moderne, a center for the art nouveau style. This
beautiful color plate is one of 24 in the portfolio *Documents de Bijouterie et Orfèvrerie
Modernes* and illustrates hatpins, belt buckles, rings, and necklaces.

37.   Sister Sarah Collins, New Lebanon, N.Y., July 1912. Silver
        gelatin print.

*SA24.1 Edward Deming Andrews Memorial Shaker Collection, gift of Edward
Deming and Faith Andrews*

Sister Sarah Collins, shown weaving a tape seat, was the last Shaker participant in
the once-thriving Shaker chair industry at their community in Mount Lebanon,
New York. Although the business did not close until 1942, an article in the
Berkshire Evening Eagle on August 13, 1933, foreshadowed its demise: "The chairs
on which Sister Sarah works are sent to the ends of the earth ... now that the old
family property has been put on the market ... Sister Sarah does not relish the idea
of stopping ... With the hands of an artist she weaves the tape in making the seats
and uses shellac in touching up the woodwork."

38.   George Christian Gebelein, design for silver teapot, Boston,
        ca. 1915. Ink and watercolor.

94x1.77 Downs Collection, gift of the Friends of Winterthur

American silversmith and antique-silver dealer George Christian Gebelein was
born in Bavaria, Germany, but had moved to Boston by the age of 14, when
he apprenticed at the firm of Goodnow & Jenks. In 1909 he opened his own
shop on Chestnut Street and specialized in custom and commissioned silver
work for individuals, universities, churches, and other businesses. Gebelein joined
the Society of Arts and Crafts, Boston, in 1903. Many of his designs

38.

were in the popular arts and crafts style or were reproductions and adaptations of American colonial silver. Above the door to his shop was hung an antique-style sign with a painted teapot and "GEBELEIN/SILVER-SMITH."

39.   Louise Brigham, *Box Furniture: How to make a Hundred Useful Articles for the Home.* New York: Century Co., 1919.

NK2408 B85 Printed Book and Periodical Collection, gift of the Friends of Winterthur

The author of *Box Furniture*, Louise Brigham studied in the Domestic Science and Domestic Art departments at Pratt Institute, New York City, and later with such influential designers as Charles Rennie Mackintosh (in Glasgow) and Josef Hoffmann (in Vienna). She perfected her ideas for transforming packing boxes into stylish domestic furniture forms from necessity while living on a remote and treeless island in the Arctic Ocean. This volume is Brigham's own copy of the 1919 printing and contains her extensive notations for a projected (but never published) future edition.

39.

40.

40.	Georges Darcy, *Or et Couleurs*. Paris: A. Calavas, 1920. Silk-screened print.

NK1535 D21 F Printed Book and Periodical Collection, gift of the Friends of Winterthur

In the 1920s the Librarie des Arts Décoratifs in Paris published a number of folios containing original designs in the newly popular art deco style for the use of decorators and designers. Although the artist of this volume, Georges Darcy, is relatively unknown, his patterns for silk-screened plates epitomize the stylized and conventionalized flora and fauna and vibrant, saturated colors characteristic of art deco.

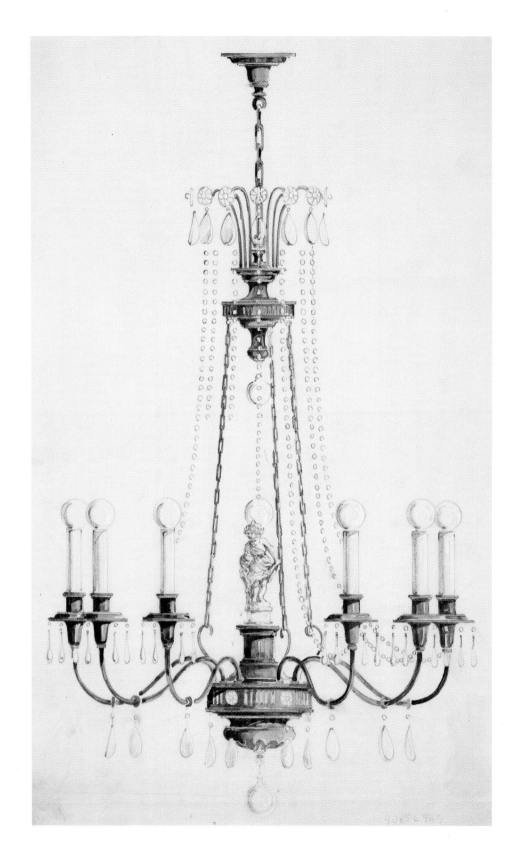

54. Georgian Lighting Shops, design for a chandelier, 1921–50s. Watercolor, gouache, and graphite.

Chapter 3

Shaping the Market: Advertising and Distribution

by Jeanne Solensky and E. Richard McKinstry

Throughout the years, whether in America or Europe, craftsmen as well as large manufacturers have used the same kinds of media to promote their products: trade catalogues, trade cards and labels, and advertising ephemera. Because of technological advances in printing, the format of these items has changed over time. Fabric swatch books, hand-drawn watercolor catalogues, and engraved labels—once considered standard—segued into colorful chromolithographed publications in the late 19th and early 20th centuries. Even so, their messages have remained resolute. Individual shopkeepers, traveling salespersons, and large manufacturing businesses have all wanted to represent their products in the best possible way.

Expositions, too, have provided manufacturers with occasions to ply their wares and customers with opportunities to comparison shop. With origins in a series of fairs that began in Paris in 1798, expositions have mirrored the development of manufacturing advances worldwide and have charted national pride through industrial achievement.

In addition, newspaper advertisements have supplied venues for both local and national advertising. Craftsmen regularly announced their merchandise to hometown residents, and larger enterprises cast wider nets by placing ads in papers in distant parts. Working for syndicates, salespersons carried cuts—illustrations of products—around the country for editors to use before the advent of the high-speed communications so common today.

Enticed to purchase from advertisements or because of a maker's reputation, both the customer and craftsman had to keep records. Early on, sellers used manuscript account books to chronicle their sales, and buyers retained invoices, some of which contained illustrative vignettes of what they had purchased. Every so often, letters clarified orders or served as a way for disputes to be settled.

Thankfully, historical documents such as the ones described here have survived the years to give us glimpses into the advertising and distribution of products from the 18th into the 20th century. Read in different ways, these documents also provide insight into everyday life in Europe and the United States. Account books always record sales, but they also tell us something about the economic conditions of their times; illustrations of goods depict specific objects, but they also inform us about the pursuit of artistic endeavors. Diaries may register work accomplishments, but they too reveal particulars about social interaction. Used in tandem with secondary documents, primary resources help clarify investigations into many and various aspects of our country's history.

41.   Catalogue of doorknobs, escutcheons, door knockers, furni-
       ture brasses, sconces, etc. England, ca. 1789. Engraving.

NK7899 B61c TC Printed Book and Periodical Collection, gift of the Friends
of Winterthur*

This trade catalogue contains patterns for brass objects in the rococo and
Adamesque styles and was originally owned by Samuel Rowland Fisher. As a partner in the Philadelphia firm of Joshua Fisher & Sons, which imported goods to
be sold to other merchants, Fisher made several trips to England to buy directly
from manufacturers. Much of the furniture hardware in the catalogue was sold to
Philadelphia cabinetmakers and can be found on several pieces of furniture
owned by Winterthur.

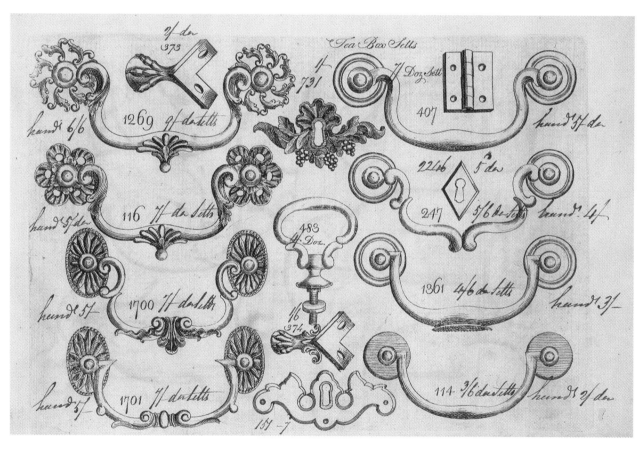

42.

42. Norwich worsted pattern book. Norwich, England, 1794–97. Iron gall ink and textiles.

65x695.3 Downs Collection, gift of the Friends of Winterthur

Swatch books such as this one provide information on English textile manufacturers in the late 18th century as well as examples of fabric imported to America before native industries produced enough goods to meet the demand. A center for worsted weaving, Norwich manufactured large quantities of this lightweight cloth that was suitable for embroidery. Callimancoes were a versatile type of worsted with a fine gloss. They came in a variety of colors and were used to make clothing, bed curtains, coverlets, and upholstery.

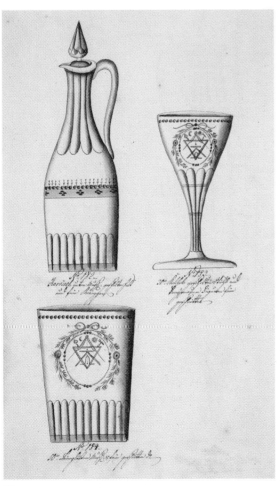

43.

43. Glass pattern book. Parchen, Bohemia, 1790–1825. Iron gall and india inks.

71x206.1 Downs Collection, gift of the Friends of Winterthur

Glassmaking factories were rare in early America. A manufacturer needed a sizeable capital investment, trained craftsmen, raw materials and fuel, and a site large enough to house everything. Consequently, imports of German and Bohemian glass were less expensive. This pattern book of ink-and-wash illustrations of decanters, goblets, pitchers, urns, and vases is possibly a compilation of wares from several manufacturers. Inscribed on one of the pages is the name of Johannes Schiefner, a resident of Parchen, Bohemia, who operated an export and commission agency in 1805. Commonly referred to as the *Gardiner's Island Glass Catalogue* after the place in New York where it was found, this volume was most likely given to an American merchant—possibly John Lyon Gardiner, who may have been involved in the importation of glass—by Schiefner or another glassware agent.

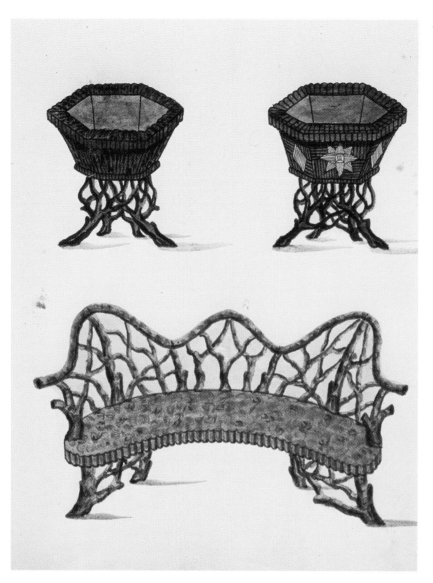

44.   T. Rutter, sketchbook. England, 1800–1850. Watercolor
        and glaze.

84x44 Downs Collection, gift of the Friends of Winterthur

In the 19th century, gardens were beginning to be thought of as extensions of the
home, and people looked for objects to outfit the areas. From 1819, when he
established his business, T. Rutter, who identified himself as a summer-house
builder, filled this particular niche by making and selling rustic-looking gazebos
and garden seats as well as grotto baskets and flower stands. His trade label, which
is affixed to the front of this colorful catalogue, notes that he was located at
Kennington Green on Cumberland Row, most likely an address in London south
of the Thames in the borough of Lambeth.

45.

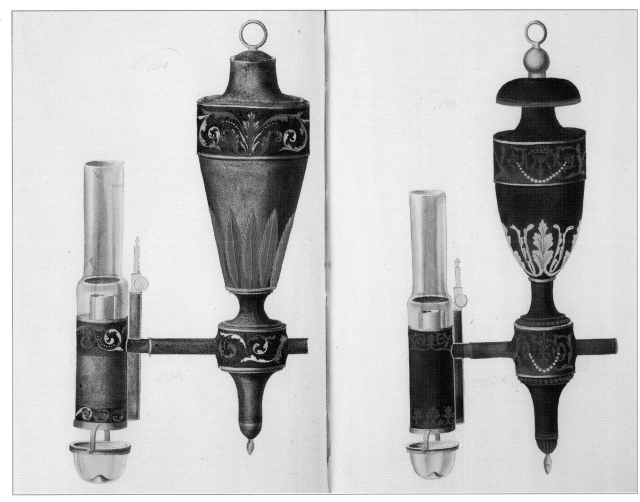

45.　　French peddler's trade catalogue. Paris, 1806–13. Watercolor and gouache.

64x68.2 Downs Collection, gift of the Friends of Winterthur

Sometime during the early years of the 19th century, a group of storekeepers in Paris banded together to produce catalogues of their wares. Choosing to hire watercolor artists instead of printers, they created at least four volumes of personal and household goods, including gloves, hats, garters, slippers, games, Argand lamps, thermometers, and fireplace bellows. Winterthur Library has volumes number one and four, identified on their spine labels as Echantillon 1 and Echantillon 4. Stationers' labels in the volumes identify a Monsieur LeBeuf, whose shop was on rue Bourg l'Abbe, as the binder. According to a contemporary city directory of Paris, all of the merchants on his street sold the kinds of goods shown in the volumes. Traditionally, historians have referred to the volumes as peddler's catalogues; however, current thought is that they may have been used on the counters in the stores along rue Bourg l'Abbe.

46.   James Barron, *Modern and Elegant Designs of Cabinet &*
        Upholstery Furniture. London: Printed by W. M. Thiselton, ca.
        1814. Hand-colored engraving.

NK7899 B27 F TC Printed Book and Periodical Collection, gift of the Friends
of Winterthur

Winterthur Library owns one of the few extant copies of this rare design catalogue. Although the title page states the creator planned to continue it annually,
Barron never fulfilled that promise. The catalogue was compiled for the general
use of cabinetmakers and upholsterers, and Barron wrote in the volume that he
realized his designs would be altered to suit changing fashions. These exquisite
hand-colored plates of sofas, beds, tables, and draperies in the Regency style
appealed to the rapidly expanding upper middle class of the early 19th century
who could afford fine furnishings and aspired to a more cultivated sensibility.

47.   G. G. Fendler & Co, toy catalogue. Nuremberg, Germany,
       1818–40. Watercolor, gouache, iron gall ink, and graphite.

*85x130 Downs Collection, gift of the Friends of Winterthur and special funds
purchase*

Toys have always been an important part of childhood, providing entertainment
and education. The household objects shown here helped to prepare children for
managing their own homes. Many toys in early America were imported from
Germany. This catalogue illustrates what items were available and how American
manufacturers were later influenced in their own production. The 135 color
plates feature mechanical toys, dolls, board games, panoramas, magic lanterns,
and miniature furniture.

48. John Thomas Smith, *The Cries of London*. London: John Bowyer Nichols and Son, 1839. Engraving.

DA688 L847a* Printed Book and Periodical Collection, gift of the Friends of Winterthur

Books of Cries have been staples of children's literature for centuries. In addition to their publication as books, Cries have been issued as broadsides, prints, playing cards, panoramas, and abecedaries. Often made with poor-quality woodcuts or engravings, they were prized by people who could not afford any other reading matter. Cries contain images and text describing people working on public streets as well as their shouts. They were intended to be educational, entertaining, and moralistic. Those that rhymed even inspired musicians and composers, including Georg Friederich Handel, who acknowledged his indebtedness. Adults collected Cries and valued their original artwork. The first Duke of Marlborough acquired 49 pen-and-ink drawings from an early edition of *The Cries of London* for his library at Blenheim Palace.

48.

49. Gillow & Co., drawing of chairs, England, ca. 1845. Ink and watercolor wash.

92x30 Downs Collection, gift of Edmond L. Lincoln

Gillow & Co., an English furnituremaking firm, established a workshop in Lancaster about 1730 and remained in business for two centuries. After opening a branch in London in 1769 and expanding its product line in 1785 to include

49.

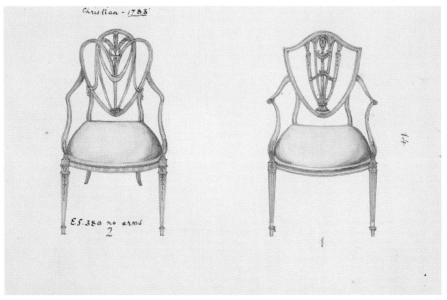

upholstery services, the small, local shop grew into a thriving national company. Gillow & Co. enjoyed much success in England with the growing middle class and abroad in the Atlantic trade. The Winterthur Library drawings show furniture, chandeliers, and draperies in a variety of styles from late Chippendale to Regency. Although some are dated 1780 to 1810, the watermarks are of a Dutch paper-making firm that began production in 1845, suggesting that these are later copies of earlier drawings.

50.   Giuseppe Capovilla, manuscript, Italy, 1848–52. Iron gall ink and watercolor.

82x269 Downs Collection, gift of the Friends of Winterthur

Not much is known about the artist Capovilla or the purpose of these designs, whether they were intended for a projected trade catalogue or as drawings for craftspeople. The ink-and-watercolor designs in the late baroque style are for Italian Roman Catholic ecclesiastical objects, such as monstrances, processional crosses, and altar fittings. Many congregations in 19th-century America chose to import furnishings for their churches directly from their native country.

50.

51. Catalogue of drawings for Japanese goods. Japan, 1860–80.
Watercolor, gouache, ink, and gilt.

75x27.1 Downs Collection, gift of the Friends of Winterthur

This catalogue of numbered drawings of porcelain, tablewares, lacquerware, vases, and furniture from the mid to late 19th century offers hints on the international trade in Japanese goods, as these objects were made specifically for exportation. The colorful and rather busy designs reflect Western tastes, and the Asian figures painted on the porcelain gave Westerners a glimpse into a foreign culture. Complementing the daintiness of the porcelain is the transparency of the tissue paper, which allows reverse images to show through.

52.

52. Roycroft Shops, *Hand Made Gifts from the Roycroft Shops.* East Aurora, N.Y.: By the shops, 1917.

Z232 R88h TC Printed Book and Periodical Collection, gift of the Friends of Winterthur

Founded by Elbert Hubbard in 1895, the Roycroft community promoted the ideals of the arts and crafts movement first through the publication of periodicals and later through catalogue sales. The Roycroft Shops marketed handcrafted items, including furniture, sculpture, carpeting, metalwork, textiles, and leather goods. During the first two decades of the 20th century, the community flourished and employed 500 "Roycrofters." However, that success did not continue. Hit hard by the death of Hubbard in the sinking of the *Lusitania* in 1915 and later by the Great Depression, the shops closed in 1938.

53. Royal Tailors, *Trade Catalogue.* Chicago: By the company, 1916.

GT1710 R88 TC Printed Book and Periodical Collection, gift of the Friends of Winterthur

The Royal Tailors company cleverly incorporated images of such figures as George Washington, Napoleon, Julius Caesar, and Walter Raleigh in this trade catalogue to showcase its guarantee of "perfection in fit, fabric, and fashion." Advertising that these distinguished men stood for quality, style, taste, and originality, Royal Tailors equated its men's clothing line with enduring virtues of the past.

George Washington wearing a Royal Tailored-to-his-order morning coat, with striped trousers.

53.

54. Georgian Lighting Shops, design for a chandelier, Philadelphia, 1921–50s. Watercolor, gouache, and graphite. *(Photo, page 30)*

90x56.469 Downs Collection, gift of Donald and Lillian Eckard

This beautiful design for a chandelier was drawn by a craftsman in the Georgian Lighting Shops of Philadelphia, a firm that operated between 1921 and the 1950s. Unfortunately, no business papers or trade catalogues have been located to provide researchers with clues about the firm. The original drawings in the Winterthur Library collection—more than 500 designs for revival-style lighting fixtures, decorative metal scrollwork, railings, and fireplace equipment—form the bulk of the firm's legacy.

55. Thomas Johnston, Lewis Deblois trade label, Boston, 1757. Copperplate engraving.

66x152 Downs Collection, gift of the Friends of Winterthur

The skilled design of this early trade card immediately commands attention. It is no surprise that the engraver, Thomas Johnston, also worked as a japanner and portrait and heraldic artist. An ornate border frames the text, which lists goods imported by Boston merchant Lewis Deblois from London, reflecting the colonists' desire for fancy goods from abroad. The reverse of the label doubled as an invoice, as was the custom.

55.

56.

56.   Henry Dawkins, Benjamin Harbeson trade label, Philadelphia, 1776. Copperplate engraving and iron gall ink.

65x708 Downs Collection, gift of Henry Francis du Pont

Trade cards, an early form of advertising, originated in London around 1700. They normally contained illustrations to inform the public of a shop's location and wares. This elaborate card for Philadelphia coppersmith Benjamin Harbeson incorporated his shop sign and images of kettles, a saucepan, and a still, all in a rococo cartouche. For this design, Henry Dawkins, an ornamental metal engraver, directly copied an English trade card engraved by E. Warner for razor-maker Henry Patten.

57.　　Elisha Babcock, Kneeland & Adams trade label, Hartford, Conn., 1793. Copperplate engraving.

67x93 Downs Collection, gift of the Friends of Winterthur

Trade labels were commonly glued to furniture pieces for authentication as well as advertising. This one for the furniture firm Kneeland & Adams, printed by Elisha Babcock, demonstrates early classical restraint with a simple rendering of the shop's furniture. The tasteful and elegant label shows an eagle on a mirror and a secretary, representing the New Republic.

58.　　E. Trenchard, Raphaelle and Rembrandt Peale trade label, Philadelphia, 1793–96. Watercolor and engraving.

71x249 Downs Collection, gift of the Friends of Winterthur

This beautifully engraved and hand-painted trade label befits the advertisers, Raphaelle and Rembrandt Peale, two of the 17 children of noted painter and scientist Charles Willson Peale. At this time, the brothers were in the early stages of their professional careers as portrait painters in Philadelphia. Raphaelle became known for his still life and trompe l'oeil paintings and scientific writings; Rembrandt for his portraits of George Washington and Thomas Jefferson. They worked tirelessly to promote the arts through the establishment of the Peale Museum of art and natural history and through Rembrandt's involvement in the Pennsylvania Academy of the Fine Arts and the American Academy of Art.

58.

59.

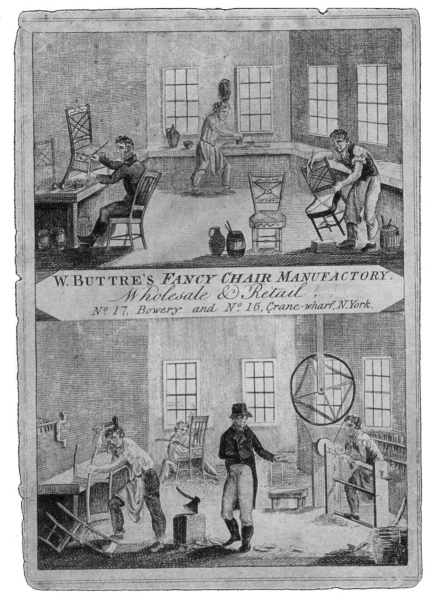

59.   William Buttre trade label, New York, ca. 1813. Wood
        engraving.

81x96 Downs Collection, gift of the Friends of Winterthur

A rare and invaluable look into the workings of a craft shop, this trade label
depicts the entire chairmaking process from the lathe-turning of parts to rush-
seat weaving to ornamental painting. William Buttre, in business in New York
City in the early 1800s, made chairs in the early federal, or neoclassical, style remi-
niscent of those from his more famous colleague Duncan Phyfe.

60.   C. E. Egelman, Peter Durand Jr. trade card, Reading, Pa., ca.
       1815. Watercolor and engraving.

64x53 Downs Collection, gift of the Friends of Winterthur

The post-Revolutionary period saw rapid growth in American manufactories as
the newly independent nation struggled to build an economy. Businessmen such
as hatmaker Peter Durand advertised their pride in their work and their country
through the use of national symbols. The bald eagle, patriotic shield, and figure
of Liberty on this trade card engraved by C. E. Egelman perfectly epitomize the
spirit and design vocabulary of the early republic.

61.

61.   Young & Delleker, Thomas Fletcher trade label,
Philadelphia, ca. 1838. Copperplate engraving.

63x13 Downs Collection, gift of the Friends of Winterthur

A Philadelphia jeweler in the early 19th century, Thomas Fletcher gained his reputation with his partner, silversmith Sidney Gardiner, for designing trophies in
commemoration of the War of 1812. Even as late as the 1830s Fletcher advertised his business with an 1822 design of a trophy urn made for Isaac Hull, a
commodore in the U.S. Navy. In addition to manufacturing plated ware, flatware,
watches, lamps, jewelry, and candlesticks, Fletcher also imported goods from
England to sell in his shop.

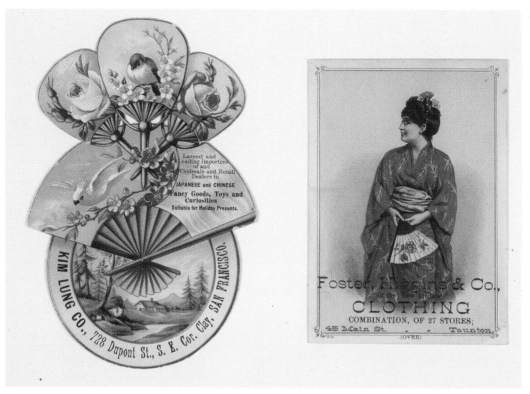

62.   Japanesque trade cards, United States, 1875–95.
        Chromolithographs.

91x108 Downs Collection, gift of the Friends of Winterthur

With the opening of Japan to trade in 1854, the American market was flooded
with goods from the Far East. In the 1870s Japanese novelty stores in major cities
carried such goods, which were also displayed at the 1876 Philadelphia Centennial
International Exhibition. The 1885 success of Gilbert and Sullivan's operetta *The
Mikado,* with the related opening of the "Japanese Village" in New York City's
Madison Square Garden (where working artisans sold their wares), exposed even
more Americans to Japanese art and design. To benefit from the craze, American
companies incorporated Japanese imagery in their advertising.

63.   E. Conrad, advertisement for F. A. Kleine, New York, 1827. Wood engraving.

58x30.2 Downs Collection, gift of the Friends of Winterthur

New Jersey, with its rich clay and access to transportation networks, was the home of numerous potteries in the 19th century, including F. A. Kleine's. Although stoneware was mostly imported to the colonies before the American Revolution, it later grew in popularity with local potters because of its durability, as illustrated in this advertisement printed by E. Conrad.

64.   Advertisement for Henry Sailor, Philadelphia, 1837–41. Steelplate engraving.

75x183 Downs Collection, gift of the Friends of Winterthur

Henry Sailor, a stonecutter in Philadelphia at 10th and Vine in the late 1830s, also crafted marble mantels, monuments, and tombstones. Edwin Greble, a contemporary who owned a marble yard in Philadelphia and whose surviving letters are at Winterthur, commented that the only way stonecutters could be successful in the tombstone trade was to be in partnership with cemetery managers or to offer them what he termed "commissions." Transitory in nature because of their ephemerality, items such as this trade label are rare. The engraving may have ornamented an invoice.

65.   Advertisement for William Gale Jr. & Co. and Brown & Spaulding, New York, 1867. Lithograph.

68x33 Downs Collection, gift of the Friends of Winterthur

The so-called joys of shopping—meandering through store displays, gazing at objects, turning desire into ownership—are extolled in this illustrated ad for two silver and jewelry stores. With the mass production of goods in the mid-1800s, home manufacturing declined, resulting in increased leisure time for the middle class. Shopping therefore was seen as a pleasurable way to while away one's free time.

66.   Peddler's license, Albany, N.Y., 1829. Iron gall ink.

80x5 Downs Collection, gift of the Friends of Winterthur

Advertisement for Culbertson's Empire Traveling Store,
New York, ca. 1870. Wood engraving.

77x410 Downs Collection, gift of the Friends of Winterthur

After the Civil War the commercial traveler—or drummer—was an increasingly
visible presence on the roads and rails that connected urban centers with small-
town America. With the advent of print advertising and America's growing industrial development, his role as a salesman was an important one. In April 1829 the
state of New York issued 21 peddler's licenses, for those who were walking or
using just one horse for transportation. By the 1870s, when dry goods merchant
J. H. Culbertson was in business, he had a wagon pulled by two horses and was
warning customers about his competition.

67.   R. M. Wagan, Philadelphia,
       1876. Albumen print.

*SA1036.1 Edward Deming Andrews
Memorial Shaker Collection,
gift of Edward Deming and Faith
Andrews*

Robert M. Wagan directed the chairmaking
enterprise at the Mount Lebanon, New
York, Shaker community where the Shaker
home ministry was located. He expanded
the business during the 1860s and 1870s by
introducing new machinery, and in 1872
the Shakers built a new factory to accom-
modate heightened demand. By 1876 the
order was in decline, but they nevertheless
took part in the Philadelphia Centennial
International Exhibition that year by show-
ing off their furnituremaking skills.

67.

68.

68.   Alden's, store exterior, Boston, 1890–99. Albumen print.

79x123.1 Downs Collection, gift of the Friends of Winterthur

Photographs of store exteriors and interiors are an invaluable tool in documenting the variety of goods offered and the displays intended to entice customers. A
storefront in Boston in the 1890s used a twist on an old tradition. Instead of a
shop sign, the owner placed a giant coffee pot near the curb and hung baskets
outside the door, announcing the type of goods he sold.

69.   Advertisement for Henry Meis, New
       York, 1890–99. Chromolithograph.

*73x319.56 Maxine Waldron Collection of Children's
Books and Paper Toys, gift of Maxine Waldron*

In a bit of whimsy or perhaps clever marketing, Henry
Meis advertised his Brooklyn house furnishings store with
a paper doll. Although he sold common goods such as
crockery and glassware, Meis may have hoped to expand
his business by attracting younger customers.

70.   Lee Kwong Kee Co. trade card,
       Kiukiang, China, ca. 1893.
       Chromolithograph.

*68x155.278 Downs Collection, gift of the
Friends of Winterthur*

69.

Although it was a year late, the 1893 World's Columbian Exposition marked the
400th anniversary of Columbus's landing in the New World. The exposition was
the largest public fair yet to be held in the United States. More than 27 million
people flocked to Chicago to see the massive temporary structures. In the grand-
est, the Manufacturers & Liberal Arts Building, domestic and foreign businesses
from all over the world advertised and exhibited their wares.

70.

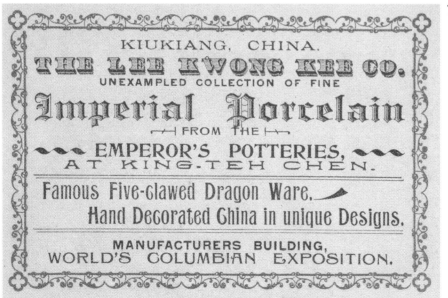

71.   Cortlandt, Billings & Co. account book, New York, 1784–86. Iron gall ink.

74x97 Downs Collection, gift of the Friends of Winterthur

The account book of the mercantile firm Cortlandt, Billings & Co. offers a glimpse into the buying habits of residents of 1780s New York City. The firm's clients included members of New York's first families—Col. Alexander Hamilton, Peter Stuyvesant, John Schuyler, Peter Ten Broeck, and the Van Cortlandts—who purchased jewelry, swords, shoes, dry goods, and groceries. Democratic in its dealings, the business also supplied local craftspeople with household goods and hardware.

72.   Samuel Williamson ledger, Philadelphia, 1810–13. Iron gall ink.

89x35.2a Downs Collection, gift of the Friends of Winterthur

Account books and ledgers are a treasure trove for those studying economics, buying practices, social and business networks, and design styles of decorative arts. A Philadelphia silversmith from 1794 to 1813, Samuel Williamson recorded information that allows us to reconstruct his business. In his shop he made, mended, and sold flatware, hollowware, and jewelry; trained craftsmen who in turn worked for him; and imported plated silver from Sheffield and Birmingham, England. His involvement in venture cargoes and trade with numerous Atlantic ports also comes to light. Speculation has it that he retired to Chester County, Pennsylvania, in 1813 due to the blockading of ports during the War of 1812, which curtailed his import/export business.

73.   Duncan Phyfe, drawing of chairs, New York, 1816. Iron gall ink and graphite.

56x6.4 Downs Collection, gift of the Friends of Winterthur

By the time of his death in 1854, Duncan Phyfe had amassed an estate appraised at $300,000. An émigré from Scotland, Phyfe opened a cabinetmaking shop in Albany, New York, in 1783 and before 1792 moved to New York City, where his thriving business operated until 1847. Phyfe's work was widely copied, and the early federal style was his greatest success. His factory employed nearly 100, among them his brothers and sons, and his customers included many of New York's leading worthies. An 1816 letter sent to Charles Bancker of Philadelphia contains sketches of new designs for chairs with corresponding prices that Phyfe most likely copied from his personal edition of a New York price book for cabinetmakers.

73.

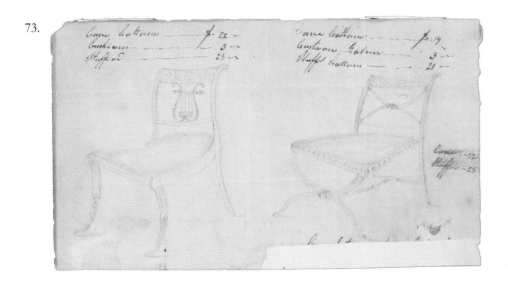

74.

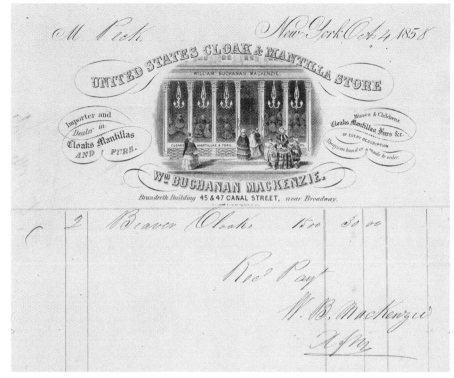

74.   Invoice for beaver cloaks, from Wm. Buchanan Mackenzie
        to M. Peck, New York, 1858. Steel engraving and iron gall
        ink.

        77x153.1 Downs Collection, gift of the Friends of Winterthur

Printed bills are important for recording the quantity and costs of goods sold and
for conveying a certain image through the use of vignettes. The scene on store-
keeper Mackenzie's bill shows a bustling street with groups of women and children inspecting the window display.

75.   John Young Taylor diary, Oswego, N.Y., 1892. Iron gall ink.

        91x53 Downs Collection, gift of the Friends of Winterthur

John Young Taylor sold "services," or illustrations, for the first newspaper syndicate in the United States, known as both the Bacheller & Johnson Syndicate and
the New York Press Syndicate. It was established by Irving Bacheller to serialize
his own literary works. The illustrations were used to improve a business's advertising. As he traveled throughout America, Taylor recorded his observations of
life on the road, the people he met, places he stayed, exchanges with businessmen,
and his dealings with the syndicate.

87. Robert and James Adam, *The Works in Architecture* …, 1779. Hand-colored engraving.

Chapter 4

Shaping the Home: Consumers and the Domestic Setting

by Neville Thompson

The ultimate focus of every designer and marketer of goods is, naturally, the consumer. Choices made by consumers with regard to their domestic setting—including architecture, landscape design, interiors, and furnishings—have been recorded throughout the years in both printed materials and photographs. Such significant resources provide us with a fascinating view of history.

Since the very early years of the printed book, architecture has been extensively documented. Volumes of architectural designs—both those projected and those completed—have had notable influences on the styles of their times. Views of buildings not only depict structures thought important in the period but may be the only remaining record of those now vanished.

In addition to architecture, gardens and landscapes of all types have been equally well published. Since gardens are even more fragile, however, treatises on garden design and embellishments are especially vital for the reconstruction of landscapes that have often changed beyond recognition.

Inevitably, the dictates of fashion have led to the rapid disappearance of original interior designs. As tastes change, so do walls, furniture, and textile furnishings. Therefore, sources that illustrate the taste in design at any one point in time are invaluable. Fashionable periodicals, design manuals, and trade catalogues all fall into this category. An equally useful resource is the record of long-gone interiors captured in photographs, which hold their own particular fascination.

But architecture, interior furnishings, and the surrounding environment cannot tell the whole story. Without the occupants and their daily lives, a household is incomplete. The interaction between people and their homes and belongings is at the heart of research into the "lives" of things. Advice, instruction, and domestic economy manuals; etiquette books; cookbooks; children's books, and other types of popular literature are particularly revealing documents.

Taken together, these all-important materials combine to illuminate the tastes of consumers, the choices they made, and the lives they created. They are indispensable components to formulating and interpreting an accurate picture of the past.

76.   Johannes Kip, *Britannia Illustrata; or, Views of all the Palaces, Several Seats, and Other Publick Buildings of England.* London: Printed by C. Dicey & Co., 172-. Hand-colored copperplate engraving.

NA7745 K 57a F Printed Book and Periodical Collection

This bird's-eye view of the great country house of Longleat, engraved after the topographical drawings of Leonard Knyff, perfectly conveys the appearance of a well-appointed estate with all its outbuildings and agricultural surroundings. Such country house portraits were to appear for centuries thereafter, embodying an ideal of English life that would be emulated in such country houses as Winterthur. Johannes Kip specialized in engravings of widely known public and private buildings. His works were collected, published, and republished throughout the 18th century.

77.   Nicholas King, *A Plan, and Perspective-View of a House and Other Buildings, Belonging to Mr. Edwd. Langley* [Washington, D.C.], 1798. Watercolor.

72x5 Downs Collection, gift of Benjamin Ginsburg

Yorkshire-born Nicholas King first appeared on the Washington scene as city surveyor, assisting in laying out lots for the infant metropolis. He was also a capable architect and watercolorist. At least two of King's completed architectural projects survive—one a grand Georgetown house, Evermay. King was an accomplished mapmaker as well, responsible for reworking the maps sent to President Thomas Jefferson by, among others, Lewis and Clark.

78.   G. van Laar, *Magazijn van Tuin-Sieraaden.* Amsterdam, Netherlands: J. de Ruyter, 1802. Hand-colored engraving.

SB471 L11 Printed Book and Periodical Collection*

Although the Netherlands may not spring to mind when the picturesque garden is mentioned, one of the most lavish compendia of such garden plans and ornament appeared there, issued by nurseryman G. van Laar. The designs were inspired by the fashionable English landscape garden, itself supposedly modeled after Chinese originals.

Amidst a welter of designs for winding pathways, Chinese pavilions, and carefully constructed hermit's caves, this plate appears—a suggestion for a preindustrial ferris wheel powered by brawn alone.

78.

79.   Henry H. Crapo, views of the Rotch House, New Bedford,
       Mass., ca. 1880. Watercolors.

69x220.2, .5 Downs Collection, gift of Mrs. John M. Bullard

The Rotch House was designed in 1845 by Alexander Jackson Davis for prominent New Bedford merchant William James Rotch. Davis was among the most
well-known and influential architects of his day, and this project perfectly exem-
plifies his Gothic-revival cottage style. When shown the design, the client's father
noted that he was "exceedingly disgusted, because it was a departure from any of
the accepted styles in New Bedford." These watercolors were executed some
decades later by Henry H. Crapo, a prominent New Bedford artist. The Rotch
House, listed in the National Register of Historic Places, still stands but has been
moved from its original site.

80.   Hans Vredeman de Vries, *Differents pourtraicts de Menuiserie.*
Antwerp, Belgium: Philippe Galle, 1588?. Engraving.

NK1115 S43 F v.1 Printed Book and Periodical Collection

These designs are said to be the earliest known printed furniture patterns, from
the hand of versatile and prolific Dutch designer Hans Vredeman de Vries. He
published numerous suites of engravings for an array of projects ranging from
garden furniture to tombs and triumphal arches. His style combined the classical
orders with the fashionable mannerist ornament that had originated in the courts
of 16th-century Italy. Such printed sources passed from hand to hand and were
copied by widening circles of craftsmen. Eventually the style spread to the middle
classes of northern Europe and would reappear as the "Pilgrim Century" furniture of 17th-century New England.

81.   Daniel Marot, *Werken van D. Marot.* Amsterdam,
       Netherlands, ca. 1707. Engraving.

NK1535 M35* Printed Book and Periodical Collection

Huguenot Daniel Marot, trained in the court workshops, fled France during the
religious turmoil of the late 17th century. In the Netherlands he designed the interiors of the royal palace of Het Loo for William III, coordinating everything from
furniture and textiles to stepped chimneypieces for the display of Chinese porcelain collected by Queen Mary. Following William to England after 1688, Marot
oversaw the furnishing of Hampton Court Palace, giving rise to the style often
known as William and Mary.

Marot's work appeared as groups of engraved prints gathered into suites, typically six plates devoted to one subject. The suites were later assembled into collections such as this volume. Winterthur's copy bears an inscription indicating that it was purchased at a sale of the effects of "Robert Freebairn" in Edinburgh in 1709. The new owner carefully indexed the entire volume by subject and numbered all of the plates consecutively.

82.

82. J. Carwitham, *Floor-Decorations of Various Kinds, Both in Plano & Perspective.* London: Sold by R. Caldwell, 1739. Engraving.

NA3840 C33 Printed Book and Periodical Collection

Printed pattern books for floor pavements were produced from the Renaissance onward. In 18th-century England, simple black-and-white checkered floors in well-to-do households were upstaged by more elaborate designs such as those in this volume. Carwitham had worked on a similar pattern book for architect Batty Langley, but his own small book is distinguished by delightful groups of figures—shepherds, dancers, commedia del l'arte characters—disporting themselves and by the dizzying proximity of flat and perspective patterns. These patterns for marble later appeared in parquet and even as painted floorcloths.

83. Catalogue of brass objects. England, 1755–1801. Engraving.

NK8360 C35c PF TC Printed Book and Periodical Collection, gift of the Friends of Winterthur

This metalwork trade catalogue is one of many produced to advertise wares from British brass founders and other artisans during the late 18th and the early 19th centuries. They stand as evidence of the British primacy in these trades. The "catalogues" are really groups of engravings carried by middlemen serving as traveling salesmen. The amazing array of household objects the catalogues offer testifies to the growing purchasing power and material aspirations of middle-class consumers.

84. William Gomm Jr., *The Side of a Drawing Room,* England, ca. 1761. Watercolor.

64x82.1 Downs Collection, gift of the Friends of Winterthur

The English cabinetmaking and upholstery firm of William Gomm & Son & Co. was a successful practitioner of mid-18th-century rococo furnishing styles. This watercolor, probably by a son of the firm's founder, is a charming record of high-style design and furniture placement in a formal drawing room of the period. This volume of Gomm materials is devoted to a variety of furniture designs and schemes for room decoration. Another at Winterthur contains drawings of the orders of architecture, and a third volume includes arithmetical exercises, a necessary skill for artisans.

85. William Ince and John Mayhew, *The Universal System of Houshold Furniture.* London, ca. 1762. Engraving.

NK2529 I36 F Printed Book and Periodical Collection, gift of Henry Francis du Pont

William Ince, trained as a cabinetmaker, and John Mayhew, apprenticed to an upholsterer, formed a partnership in 1759. From the start they assembled the designs that would appear in this compendium, a form of advertisement that was published in both French and English. They drew inspiration from their contemporary Thomas Chippendale and even shared the same engraver, the talented Matthew Darly. *The Universal System* appeared in one edition only and remains scarce to this day. It may come as a surprise to learn that the term *sofa bed* came into common usage in the 18th century, referring to an easily portable and convertible furniture form, as seen here.

85.

86.   Jean Pillement, *Recueil de Differents Panneaux Chinois Inventé et Dessiné par Jean Pillement*. Paris: Leviez, 177-. Engraving.

Printed Book and Periodical Collection, gift of Edmond L. Lincoln

Designer Jean Pillement, son of a textile designer of Lyon, created a distinctive style of rococo chinoiserie that is permanently linked to his name. It was adopted by artisans in every medium from textiles to wallpaper to furniture marquetry. Pillement's playful vision of the East was spread throughout Europe through his numerous engraved ornament suites and peripatetic professional career. The lighthearted fantasy on Chinese motifs seen here is typical of Pillement's style, which was never intended as an accurate reflection of Chinese life.

87.   Robert and James Adam, *The Works in Architecture of Robert & James Adam. v.2, Number 1: Containing Part of the Earl of Derby's House in Grosvenor-Square*. London: Printed for the authors and sold by Peter Elmsley, 1779. Hand-colored engraving. *(Photo, page 56)*

NA997 A21 v.2 PF Printed Book and Periodical Collection

Works in Architecture is justly celebrated as one of the most influential publications of its day. An elegantly illustrated compilation of the competed projects of the Scottish-born Adam brothers, it served as a prospectus for future patrons. That the brothers prided themselves on their ability to orchestrate all of the elements of a building, from roofing to lighting fixtures, is apparent in what they chose for inclusion in the volume. Winterthur's copy is one of a few surviving examples with hand-colored plates, which were available at added expense. The authors stated that this was done so that "posterity might be able to judge with more accuracy concerning the taste of the present age."

88.   George Washington, record of purchases for the president's residence in New York City, New York, 1789–96.

65x571 Downs Collection

The beautiful, legible handwriting on this list is that of George Washington, who methodically set forth an inventory of all the household furnishings purchased for his official residence. The list provides a detailed record of the goods felt necessary for fitting out a well-appointed house of the period as well as their source and prices. Similar inventories exist for Mount Vernon, testifying to the organizational skills that served Washington so well.

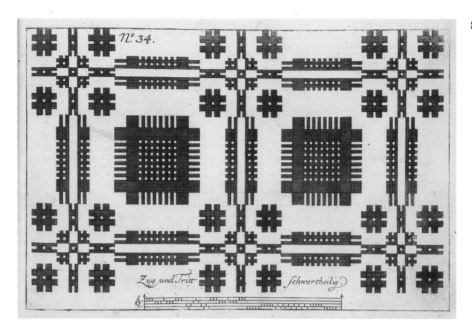

89.   Johann Michael Kirschbaum, *Neues Bild- und Muster-Buch.*
        Heilbronn, Germany: Printed by Johann Daniel Class, 1793.
        Woodcut.

TS1490 K61* Printed Book and Periodical Collection

Johann Kirschbaum was a master linen weaver in his native Germany, and this
volume was intended to be used as patterns for linen damask. The book first
appeared in 1771 and was republished as late as 1854, making it one of the most
influential and widely owned examples of such design books. Winterthur's copy,
said to have a history of ownership in central Pennsylvania, probably served as a
design source for the handsome blue-and-white double-weave woolen coverlets
so often collected today.

90.   John Jacques?, *Pattern Book of Chimney Pieces, Moldings,*
        Pilasters, etc. London, ca. 1794. Engraving.

NK1530 P31 F TC Printed Book and Periodical Collection

For those who could not afford marble mantelpieces, composition (plaster) ornament applied to wooden fireplace surrounds and overmantels constituted an
acceptable alternative. Such ornament was sold by the piece or by the yard, allowing a designer to create an original grouping to the owner's taste. This catalogue
of composition ornament, a rare survival, has been ascribed to London carver
and gilder John Jacques, whose firm did considerable business in such material in
the 1790s. Jacques seems to have purveyed the full range of design motifs made
popular by the Adam brothers for their wealthy clientele.

90.

91.   *Magasin für Freunde des Guten Geschmacks*. Leipzig, Germany:
       Friedrich August Leo, 1796. Hand-colored engraving.

NK1160 M18 Printed Book and Periodical Collection

Chinoiserie was not the only exotic decorative style to appeal to Western tastes, as
this handsome plate demonstrates. The *Magasin für Freunde* is what we would now
call a shelter magazine, offering a menu of handsomely presented design ideas for
client and architect. This issue also contains ideas for Pompeiian, pastoral, and
Roman room settings. In this plate, what the taste of the time called *turqueries*,
several Islamic motifs are combined into an interior "in the Turkish taste,"
complete with a *divan*, a furniture form of Eastern origin. The designer, German
architect J. G. Klinsky, has concocted a delectable fantasy setting for an adventur-
ous patron.

91.

92.   *The Cabinet-Makers' Philadelphia and London Book of Prices.*
       Philadelphia: Printed by Snowden & McCorkle, 1796.

   NK 2406 P54a Printed Book and Periodical Collection

Price books issued by associations of furnituremakers and other artisans are invaluable documents for the history of the trade, records of consumer taste, and availability and cost of household objects at specific points in time. This volume lists the prices for furniture in Philadelphia in 1796, based on those from the London price book of 1793 with a surcharge added for this country. The book cites a specific form and the additional costs for enhancements. By the 1840s such sources disappeared, as competition between individual artisans and the advent of mass production rendered price-fixing obsolete.

   This edition is an important document in labor history. It came at the end of a two-year struggle over work-related issues between masters and journeymen in the Philadelphia furniture trade. The preface records the final agreement between the groups. Both front cover and bookplate in Winterthur's copy note its ownership by William Sinclair, a cabinetmaker from Flowertown, Pennsylvania, and a member of the Society of Journeyman Cabinetmakers.

93.   Gaetano Landi, *Architectural Decorations.* London: By the author, 1810. Hand-colored engraving.

   NK1535 L25 PF Printed Book and Periodical Collection, gift of Edmond L. Lincoln and the Friends of Winterthur

This volume is a paradox. It is a collection of printed suites of designs for interiors, furniture, and decorative objects in a range of historic and exotic styles, rendered in a most accomplished manner, carefully hand colored, and sumptuous in every way—by an artist-designer about whom almost nothing is known. The little that *is* known about Landi is intriguing. He was a friend of eminent English architect John Soane, as their correspondence testifies, but Landi's ambitions apparently outran his resources. One of his letters to Soane announces that he is leaving for Russia and asks for a loan. After this, nothing more is known of him.

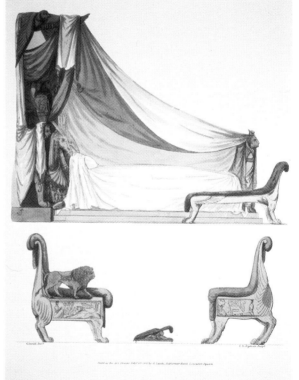

93.

94.   Désiré Guilmard, *Album Gothique: Recueil de Meubles et de Sièges.* Paris: By the author, 185-.

NK2390 G96 Printed Book and Periodical Collection

Prolific Parisian publisher Désiré Guilmard was responsible for spreading French taste in furniture and interiors to a worldwide audience through his numerous and varied publications. He is best known for the journal *Le Garde-Meuble*—which for half a century was circulated wherever cabinetmakers sought inspiration—and for his important work on printed sources of ornament design, *Les Maîtres Ornemanistes.* Unlike much of the furniture illustrated by Guilmard, the Gothic-revival designs in this small volume may have been designed by the author himself.

95.   *Gothic Album for Cabinet Makers: Comprising a Collection of Designs for Gothic Furniture.* Philadelphia: Henry Carey Baird, 1868. Engraving.

NK2345 G68 Printed Book and Periodical Collection

It is immediately apparent that this album of furniture designs is a line-for-line copy of Désiré Guilmard's *Album Gothique* of the 1850s; only the captions have been changed. However, Guilmard's name appears nowhere in the volume. This re-publication by the well-known Baird firm of Philadelphia does demonstrate one way in which design ideas were spread, even though this style was out of fashion by 1868.

96.   Auguste Racinet, *L'Ornement Polychrome.* Paris: Firmin-Didot, ca. 1872. Chromolithograph.

NK1530 R11 F Printed Book and Periodical Collection

The introduction of chromolithography in the 19th century made the publication of colorplate books possible in greater numbers for a lower price. Among those quick to realize the opportunities were compilers of illustrated encyclopedias of ornament, most notably Owen Jones, whose 1856 *Grammar of Ornament* led the way. These compilations served as mines of ideas for designers of all kinds. By the time Auguste Racinet issued his own dazzling collection, printing in gold and silver inks had been perfected, allowing for even greater visual punch. Racinet explains that the designs so artfully combined in this plate were taken from the decoration of Indian weapons exhibited in 1869 at a Parisian exposition of industrial arts.

96.

97.   Belcher Mosaic Glass Company, *Trade Catalogue*. New York: By the company, 1886. Hand-colored plate.

NK5399 B42 TC Printed Book and Periodical Collection

This stained-glass window design, marketed when residential stained glass was much in vogue, was produced by a New York company that had sold window glass for decades. In 1884 and 1885 the Belcher Company took out patents on "mosaic glass," for which triangular-shape glass pieces were a key element. They produced this sumptuous catalogue of ecclesiastical and residential designs with hand-colored plates and an introduction by well-known art critic Caryl Coleman. This window appeared at the height of the aesthetic movement, a style greatly influenced by the arts of Japan. The popularity of Belcher's designs, and of stained glass in the home, was not to last, and the firm went out of business not long afterward. Some Belcher glass installations have survived; their distinctive style makes them immediately recognizable.

98.	Theodore Newton Vail, *Mine Own House*. Roxbury, Mass.: Privately published, 1887.

F74 R88v F Printed Book and Periodical Collection

Photography allowed the house-proud owner of the 19ᵗʰ century to pioneer a new sub-genre of vanity publishing—the lavishly produced, privately printed photographic record capturing one's home in every detail. Theodore Vail, an entrepreneur of the robber baron era, created this volume, covering his house and grounds from stable to attic, even the family dog! With such plates as guides, late Victorian interiors can be recaptured down to the last inkwell and teaspoon.

99.	Anderson Galleries, *Estate Sale of Theodore N. Vail, May 1–2, 1922*. New York, 1922.

Printed Book and Periodical Collection, Auction Catalogue Collection

In the natural order of things, household belongings are amassed and dispersed, to the ongoing delight of antiques dealers and collectors. This particular catalogue records the sale of effects carefully gathered by the Vail family and illustrated in Theodore Vail's *Mine Own House*. Many entries in the catalogue can be paired with objects shown in the book. Such sale catalogues have become valuable tools for tracing the history of collections as well as their rise or fall in value.

100.	By/for Mary Harrod Northend, Mrs. Chafee's boudoir, 19–. Silver gelatin print.

99x71.6 Downs Collection, gift of the Friends of Winterthur

Mary Harrod Northend, a journalist working at the turn of the 20ᵗʰ century, is said to have amassed a collection of more than 30,000 photographs, principally of old homes and their furnishings. Northend used these to illustrate her many books and articles on the subject, often centering on her native New England. Some of the photographs were taken by Northend herself, others by professional photographers under her direction. According to an inscription on this image, the boudoir is that of "Mrs. Chafee, with art treasures secured by General Chafee during his military service in China." The room demonstrates yet another Westerner's fascination with the arts of the East.

101.

101.   Jessie Tarbox Beals, sitting room at White Pines,
        Woodstock, N.Y., 19–. Platinum print.

92x39.1140.249 Downs Collection, gift of Mark and Jill F. Willcox

White Pines, the home of Ralph Radcliffe Whitehead and his wife, Jane Byrd
McCall Whitehead, was the centerpiece of Byrdcliffe, their ambitious arts and
crafts colony outside Woodstock, New York. Founded in 1901, the colony did not
last long in its original form, but the Whiteheads continued to entertain streams
of visitors over the years. Among them was pioneer woman photojournalist Jessie
Tarbox Beals, who recorded the interiors of a dwelling consciously designed and
furnished to the strict precepts of the arts and crafts movement.

102.   Clara Andrews Williams, *The House That Glue Built*. New
        York: Frederick A. Stokes, ca. 1905. Colored plate.

Z1033 W72 Printed Book and Periodical Collection*

Many turn-of-the-century girls kept scrapbooks, but a few turned these into
virtual two-dimensional dollhouses, creating room settings out of wallpaper
samples, illustrations from mail-order catalogues, and newspaper advertisements—in effect, practicing the fitting-out of their own homes in the years to
come. Publishers eventually seized on the idea, offering handsome picture books

with plates of rooms ready to furnish and populate using scissors, glue, and pages of families, pets, and household objects. What distinguishes this volume are the authentic and stylish arts and crafts furnishings, offering lessons in taste even to the young consumer.

103.   A. A. Vantine and Company, *Catalogue: The Oriental Store.*
       New York: By the company, 1914.

NK1133 V28 TC Printed Book and Periodical Collection, gift of the Friends of Winterthur

The long-lived Vantine firm prospered for many years from its import business, featuring decorative goods from every corner of Asia. Its seven-story New York retail store lured customers with exotic room settings and sold everything from sets of porcelain dinnerware to Japanese lanterns at affordable prices and through the mail. Vantine exemplified the democratization of the taste for the exotic. One customer whose receipt survives, Mrs. Samuel L. Clemens of Hartford, Connecticut, no doubt wished to accessorize the fashionable interiors of her house with appropriate oriental bibelots.

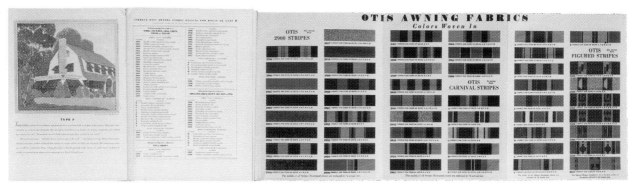

104.   Otis Company, *Awnings: A Guide to Their Selection.* New York:
        By the company, ca. 1930.

NA3008 O88 TC Printed Book and Periodical Collection, gift
of Claire W. Nagle*

Long before air conditioners, there were awnings. By the 1930s they had been in
use for many years. This lavish volume from the Otis Company goes far beyond
a simple display of available awning fabrics and style options. The company pres-
ents a parade of the most popular house styles of the day (designed by well-
known architects), discusses their individual architectural personalities, and
recommends those awning fabrics most suited to each design. As an added
inducement, samples of fabric are included.

105.   Leslie P. Potts, *Readbourne Room*, Winterthur, Del., 1943.
        Watercolor.

WF C177 Winterthur Archives

Leslie Potts was the superintendent of Winterthur Farms during the years that
H. F. du Pont was enlarging and furnishing the house that was to become today's
Winterthur Museum. For du Pont, Potts produced a series of handsome room
plans, detailing the exact placement of furniture (located by brass markers set into
the floor, matching each furniture leg) as well as major decorative elements such
as rugs or lamps. Not only do these watercolor drawings record one person's
specific taste in home decoration, they stand as elegant and evocative renderings
in their own right. Readbourne Parlor, a room from an 18th-century Maryland
house, is now furnished with Boston japanned furniture and Philadelphia chairs.

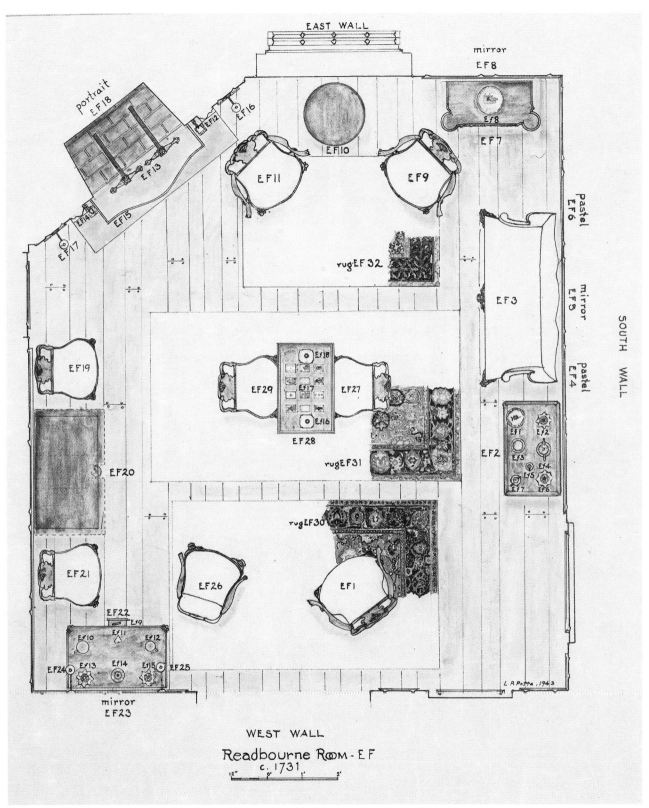

EAST WALL

mirror
EF8

portrait
EF18

EF12

EF16

EF13

EF8

EF7

EF11

EF10

EF9

EF14

EF15

pastel
EF6

EF17

rug EF32

EF3

mirror
EF5

SOUTH WALL

EF19

pastel
EF4

Ef18

EF1

EF2

EF29

Ef17

EF27

Ef3

Ef4

EF20

Ef16

Ef5

Ef6

EF28

Ef7

rug EF31

EF21

rug EF30

EF22

Ef9

Ef10

Ef11

Ef12

EF26

EF1

Ef13

Ef14

Ef15

EF24

EF25

L.P.Potts, 1943

mirror
EF23

WEST WALL

Readbourne Room - EF
c. 1731

12"   0'   1'   2'

105.

106.

106. François Nivelon, *The Rudiments of Genteel Behavior*. London, 1737. Engraving.

BJ1871 N73 Printed Book and Periodical Collection, gift of the Friends of Winterthur

François Nivelon, the author of this manual on the etiquette of the minuet, was a French émigré dancingmaster and former performer in France and England—one of the informal ambassadors of the taste for things French that was beginning to permeate many aspects of English upper-class culture at this time. Begun as a lively French country dance, the minuet had become an art of stately and carefully calibrated movement. It is clear from these engravings and their accompanying instructions that every gesture was part of a performance intended to convey specific ideas of style and class. The engraver of these plates, François Boitard, was French by birth and English by adoption. The artist, Bartholomew Dandridge, was an English portrait painter.

107. Eliza Smith, *The Compleat Housewife: or, Accomplish'd Gentlewoman's Companion*. Williamsburg, Va.: Printed and sold by William Parks, 1742.

TX705 S64 1742 Printed Book and Periodical Collection, gift of Henry Francis du Pont

This so-called Williamsburg cookbook is the first cookbook to be published in America although not the first to be written here. It is probably an unauthorized reprint of the fifth edition of a popular London work that appeared in 1727 and went through at least 18 early English editions. As is typical of such manuals, the instructions seem casual, and the extensive medical section testifies to a day when the mistress of the household was the only physician within easy reach. For such a popular work, it is surprising that little is known of its author, although she does state that her recipes are based on practical experience. Winterthur's well-used copy, in a Williamsburg binding, bears the signature and date of its probable first purchaser, Jane Williams, 1743.

108. *An Explanation and Translation of a Modern Bill of Fare, May 1751.* London: Printed for C. Mushroom Truffle Morelle in Spittre a Field, 1751.

TX727 E96* Printed Book and Periodical Collection

In the July 1751 issue of the London *Gentleman's Magazine,* a line appeared among the monthly listings of newly published books: "An explanation and translation of a modern bill of fare. *6d.*" That notice and a similar one in *Edinburgh Magazine* were, until a few years ago, the only evidence of this volume's existence. Winterthur's copy surfaced in a group of books from the du Pont family library, with no clue as to its previous history. This work is a significant document for a turning point in taste. In lighthearted terms it describes and interprets a dinner in the new French cuisine that was just becoming the mode among English upper classes and was still viewed with suspicion in some quarters.

109.

109. Ephrata Cloister, *Paradisisches Wunder-Spiel,* Ephrata, Pa., 1754. Hand-illuminated drawing.

65x560 Downs Collection, gift of Henry Francis du Pont

Ironically, collectors today feverishly seek handsome, beautifully made objects produced by members of ascetic religious communities—objects that were created by artisans who deliberately rejected the things of this world. Such were the printed books and manuscript hymnals of Ephrata Cloister in eastern Pennsylvania. The Protestant order is known today for some of the finest German-language printing in early America. Less well known are their hand-illuminated hymnal decorations, such as this vision of the Resurrection in which pre-Reformation artistic techniques are united with an ecstatic Protestant vision.

110.   Protestant Episcopal Church, *Book of Common Prayer*.
        Philadelphia: Printed by Hall and Sellers, 1785.

*BX5943 P96 s Printed Book and Periodical Collection, gift of Henry
Francis du Pont*

One effect of the American Revolution was to sever the Episcopal Church in the
United States from its status as an arm of the Established Church of Great
Britain. As a result, a committee of churchmen in this country produced a new
version of the *Book of Common Prayer*, with alterations (such as removing the
prayer for the health of the king). The prayer book was intended to be appropriate for American citizens and to convince their British counterparts of the valid-
ity of the new sister church. A number of copies were handsomely bound and
sent to the bishops of Great Britain. Winterthur's volume, according to an
inscription, was presented to the Bishop of Llandaff, Wales. The Philadelphia
binder was immigrant Caleb Buglass of Berwick-on-Tweed.

111.   John Lewis Krimmel, sketchbook, Philadelphia, 1819.
        Watercolor.

59x5.5 Downs Collection, gift of the Friends of Winterthur

The seven volumes of watercolor sketches of landscapes, townscapes, and everyday people and things left by immigrant German artist John Lewis Krimmel

111.

testify to his boundless fascination with the look and feel of his adopted country. A Philadelphia resident, Krimmel drowned at an early age, cutting short a promising career. Although he is celebrated as one of this country's earliest genre painters, Krimmel's watercolors exhibit a freshness and immediacy that the oil paintings cannot match. Leaf after leaf of the sketchbooks capture exact moments in time and place, including the first visual record of a Christmas tree in this country.

112.   Francis D. Nichols, *A Guide to Politeness*. Boston: Printed by Lincoln & Edmands, 1810. Hand-colored engraving.

GV1763 N62 s Printed Book and Periodical Collection, gift of the Friends of Winterthur

Boston dancingmaster Francis Nichols, in this charming manual on ballroom etiquette, attempted to define the rules of gentility much as his predecessor François Nivelon had a century earlier. Manuals on dance and ballroom behavior would continue to appear throughout the century, as ever greater numbers of anxious party-goers turned to them for guidance. Nichols's little book remains one of the most captivating, opening our eyes to a Boston of pleasure, reflecting the frivolity of Regency society in London.

113.   Solomon Kuder, *Der Praktische Familien-Farber*. Allentown, Pa.: Printed by Blumer, Leisenring and Co., 1858.

TP897 K95 s Printed Book and Periodical Collection

Solomon Kuder (or Kuter) of Trexlertown, Pennsylvania, was a schoolteacher, grocery store owner, and jacquard coverlet weaver. At a time when many rural households still produced their own textiles, manuals for dyeing with easily obtained materials were common. Some, such as this, included samples of the finished product. The publication was in German, probably still the primary language for Kuder and his intended audience, who, according to his preface, were the "industrious and economical" Pennsylvania German housewives who wished to do their own dyeing. The volume also includes recipes for soap, ink, and black hair dye.

116. M. [Pierre-Augustin] Salmon, *Art du Potier d'Etain*, 1788. Engraving.

Chapter 5

Revealing the Meaning: Placing Objects in Context

by Lois Olcott Price

From the Winterthur Library collections, a diverse body of material can be brought to the study and interpretation of any single object. In return, the information amassed about a body of objects informs a scholar's understanding of the society that made, sold, and used those objects. Within such a dynamic synergy lies the strength of the Winterthur Library, guiding its collecting policy as well as its unflagging commitment to education.

Whether a tankard or a teapot, drinking vessels and their contents often play a role that extends far beyond their immediate function. Such was the case in 18th-century Europe and America, when design, decoration, and use carried a particular cultural significance. Two examples from the Winterthur Museum collection—a pewter tankard and a stoneware teapot—and numerous volumes from the Winterthur Library serve to illustrate the intricate and fascinating path of discovery.

Beginning with clues provided by the objects themselves, such as a maker's mark on the tankard or the embossed decoration and unusual shape of the teapot, primary sources from the period each reveal a cultural connection. For the tankard, an artisan's daybook and a French encyclopedia offer different facets of a pewterer's business and craft. A well-documented travel account enlightens us about the consumers who purchased and used tankards. And an early treatise on cider informs us of the new and improved methods for producing the liquid found within such a vessel. For the unusual camel teapot, illustrations of real and mythological beasts and a design book of oriental images suggest sources for the novel shape. A collection of copperplate engravings commissioned by the owner of a pottery traces the entire earthenware manufacturing process, from preparation of the clay to shipment of the final product. And a small volume by a French entrepreneur eulogizing the beneficial effects of tea and the accoutrements necessary for its preparation elucidates his marketing strategies.

These rare and beautiful documents, each with a history and cultural significance of its own, speak to us of the objects created in the time and space they shared. They are the tools that allow us to understand the how, when, and why.

114.   Henry Will, tankard, New York, 1761–93. Pewter.

1965.2752 Bequest of Henry Francis du Pont

114.

This tankard was made by Henry Will, a German-born pewterer who worked in New York from 1761 until 1793. He began and ended his career in New York City but spent the years 1775 to 1783 in Albany, where the tankard was probably made. New Yorkers had a pronounced affection for tankards, documented by a significant number of surviving examples. The simple, flat lid and barrel-shape body is a 17th-century design that continued to be produced in New York throughout the 18th century.

In a society known for its prodigious consumption of hard cider, beer, and malt liquors, expensive drinking vessels played an important role. Pewter was valued as a luxury item, and a lidded tankard established the status of the owner and protected his beverage from insects and other foreign matter.

Pewter is composed of tin, lead, and other metals. A pewterer melted the ingredients before casting the parts in molds, refining the shapes on a lathe, and then soldering them together. After a final polishing, most pewterers marked their wares to identify the maker and sometimes the quality of the metal.

115.   Henry Will account book, 1763–96. Iron gall ink.

95x1.1 Downs Collection, gift of the Museum of Early Southern Decorative Arts

Although few account books have survived from the 18th century, most craftsmen used them to record business transactions. Such volumes provide clues to style, form, cost, clientele, cash flow, and related enterprises. For instance, Will's account with Asher Myers reveals the cost of a tankard (5 shillings) and indicates that Will also mended pewter. It states that Myers paid Will primarily in old pewter (melted to make new), lead (a component of pewter), and bartered services. Rare survivals such as this volume provide scholars with a glimpse into the life and times of early American craftsmen.

116.   M. [Pierre-Augustin] Salmon, *Art du Potier d'Etain*. Paris: Chez Moutard, 1788. Engraving. *(Photo, page 82)*

NK8404 S17 F Printed Book and Periodical Collection, gift of the Friends of Winterthur

The Henry Will tankard is a technically demanding form that would have passed through each of the steps illustrated by Salmon, who appears to have been a pewterer in Chartres. *Art du Potier d'Etain*, with engravings by Pierre Nicholas Ransonnette, was the final section of *Descriptions des Arts et Métiers,* a series of publications issued between 1761 and 1788 by the Academie Royale des Sciences, which sought to record the details of every industrial process in France. Although Diderot's *Encyclopédie* was better known, the text of the Academie series provided more complete descriptions. The 81 sections were issued as separate *cahiers,* which were later bound in various orders and groupings. Surviving sets, such as Winterthur's, are rare.

117.   Peter Kalm, *Travels into North America*. London: Printed
        by T. Lowndes, 1772.

E162 K14 Printed Book and Periodical Collection

Peter Kalm was a naturalist. At the suggestion of Linnaeus, he was sent to North America by the Swedish Academy of Sciences in 1748. Although his primary assignment was the collection of plant specimens potentially useful in the Nordic climate, Kalm's reports, first published in Swedish, also include observations of the people, customs, and communities he visited. He wrote one of the most useful and detailed travel accounts of the colonial period.

Kalm's journey took him to the Hudson River valley and Albany, where the Henry Will tankard was probably made. In Albany he found a conservative and frugal people who still embraced Dutch customs, language, and architecture, which may explain their preference for an early style of tankard long out of fashion in more sophisticated areas. Kalm also noted the abundance of apple orchards in the area and the excellent cider they produced—cider that probably once filled the Henry Will tankard.

117.

118.   John Worlidge, *Vinetum Britannicum; or, A Treatise of Cider.*
        London: Printed for Thomas Dring, 1678. Engraving.

Hard cider was a common beverage consumed by all classes of society in Britain
and colonial America at all hours of the day. Aside from cultivation of the apples,
the key steps in hard cider production involved crushing the fruit, pressing the
juice, and then fermenting and aging that juice. Vessels such as the Henry Will
tankard were used for consuming beverages like cider. John Worlidge wrote this
treatise in an effort to improve the quality and thereby increase the consumption
of cider as well as similar beverages made from fruit.

118.

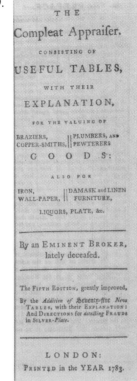

119.

119. *The Compleat Appraiser Consisting of Useful Tables, with Their Explanation for the Valuing of Braziers, Coppersmiths, Plumbers, and Pewterers Goods.* London, 1783.

TP860 P71 Printed Book and Periodical Collection

The Compleat Appraiser, a guide to estate appraisal, provides detailed instructions for identifying and valuing different grades of pewter. Such information has helped with the interpretation and verification of pewterers' hallmarks. The composition of the metal used to make pewter varied widely. The highest grade (hard-metal) resembled silver and was generally marked with a crowned X. Trifle- and lay-metal were progressively coarser in appearance and were unmarked.

120.

120. Maker's marks on Henry Will pewter tankard, New York, 1761–93.

1965.2752 Bequest of Henry Francis du Pont

The tankard is not marked with a crowned X.

121. Maker's marks on Henry Will pewter hot water plate, New York, 1761–83.

1973.0343 Museum purchase

The hot water plate carries a crowned X mark.

An XRF analysis of the Henry Will tankard was undertaken by Winterthur's Scientific Research and Analytical Laboratory to determine its chemical composition. This spectra reveals that the tankard, which is not marked with a crowned X, contains approximately 91% tin, 5% lead, 3% antimony, and trace amounts of copper. When these data are compared to that from pewter objects marked with a crowned X, clear differences emerge. Higher-quality pieces, such as the Henry Will hot water plate, contain 96–97% tin, about 1% lead, 1.5% antimony, and traces of copper.

121.

122.   Teapot, Staffordshire, England, 1745–60. Salt-glaze
        stoneware.

1958.0903 Bequest of Henry Francis du Pont

Staffordshire is well known for its potteries, which produced huge quantities of wares for export to Europe and the American colonies during the mid-18th century. The potteries drew inspiration for their designs from current fashions, particularly the infatuation with all things oriental. Because tea came from China, teapots, cups, and caddies were frequently designed in the taste known as chinoiserie. Playful, exotic shapes were common. Design and travel books often provided ideas and specific patterns.

After its introduction in England about 1650, tea became a popular and expensive beverage consumed by the upper class on social occasions. The tea equipage—pot, cups, caddy, sugar bowl, creamer, and tongs—was commonly made of silver or imported Chinese porcelain. Familiarity with the etiquette of taking tea became a symbol of gentility and social acceptance. By the mid-18th century, tea had become a more common and less costly beverage, but the aura of gentility, supported by proper etiquette and accoutrements, remained. Less expensive teapots such as this stoneware camel then flooded the market.

122.

123.   Edward Topsell, *The History of Four-footed Beasts and Serpents.*
London: Printed by E. Cotes for G. Sawbridge, 1658.
Woodcut.

QL41 T67* Printed Book and Periodical Collection

Images of exotic animals fascinated the public and inspired designs such as the camel-shape teapot. Edward Topsell's volume is a compromise between fable and biology. The delightful woodcut illustrations include familiar beasts such as the donkey and exotic animals such as dragons, hydras, and camels. Fanciful and morally instructive fables about the animals are jumbled with practical instructions on feeding and the treatment of diseases.

The volume consists of three parts. The first is drawn largely from Konrad Gesner, *Historica animalium.* The second, *The History of Serpents; or, The Second Book of Living Creatures,* was written by Topsell. The third section is a translation of Thomas Moffet, *Insectorum … theatrum* and was a popular design source for needlework and crewel patterns in the 18th century. Plates from some copies of the book have been pricked and pounced to transfer images for needleworking.

123.

124.   John Stalker and George Parker, *A Treatise on Japanning and Varnishing*. Oxford, England, 1688. Engraving.

TP938 S78 F Printed Book and Periodical Collection, gift of Henry Francis du Pont

This manual was written at the height of England's fascination with the Orient. The importation of lacquer screens, dishes, cabinets, and decorative boxes, particularly from Japan, began in the 16th century. With increasing demand and the sudden termination of trade with Japan in the early 17th century, European craftsmen developed their own version of lacquer, known as japanning. Designs influenced by those in this manual appear in almost every media, from textiles to ceramics. The top image on the plate seen here provides a clear source for the embossed design ornamenting the howdah on the camel teapot.

Stalker and Parker give detailed instructions for creating japanned images on almost any substrate as well as related information on gilding and varnishing pictures and prints and staining wood, ivory, and horn. Little is known about the authors except that they lived and worked in London and were probably skilled craftsmen familiar with the process.

124.

125.

125. Enoch Wood, *A Representation of the Manufacturing of Earthenware*. London: Ambrose Cuddon, 1827. Engraving.

TP807 R42 S Printed Book and Periodical Collection

Commissioned by Enoch Wood, proprietor of a pottery manufactory in Staffordshire, this volume contains 21 captioned copperplate engravings tracing the entire manufacturing process from preparation of the clay to the packing and shipping of the final product. The frontispiece illustrates a busy pottery yard with active kilns in the background and tourists in the foreground. The camel teapot was produced in a manufactory like this. Wood was the first to form and exhibit a collection of Staffordshire pottery, which visitors would have seen at his Fountain Place Works, a museum that was described as "altogether *unique*." This book appears to have been produced as a souvenir for visitors to the pottery and was a gift to Louisa Lovett Mitchell from her uncle in 1831.

AN ADDRESS

TO THE

YOUNG INHABITANTS

OF

THE POTTERY,

BY

JOSIAH WEDGWOOD, F.R.S.

POTTER TO HER MAJESTY.

Printed at *Newcastle*, by J. SMITH.

126.

126. Josiah Wedgwood, *An Address to the Young Inhabitants of the Pottery*. Newcastle, England: Printed by J. Smith, 1783.

NK4335 W39a S Printed Book and Periodical Collection, gift of Henry Francis du Pont

Josiah Wedgwood is known as one of England's most creative and successful potters, but he was also an innovative, early industrialist who replaced inefficient craft practices with a paternalistic factory system. After a riot precipitated by food shortages, Wedgwood addressed his workers and issued this pamphlet, pointing out the folly of using violence to effect change and extolling the positive advances that had been made in the workers' housing, wages, and lives. In Wedgwood's factories, punctuality, quality control, cleanliness, and the avoidance of waste were strictly enforced. These changes, just beginning in the Staffordshire potteries when the camel teapot was made, improved the product as well as the ability to create more complex and sophisticated wares at a profit.

127.   Nicholas de Blegny, *Le Bon Usage du The, du Caffe, et du Chocolat Pour la Preservation & Pour la Guerison de Maladies.* Lyon, France: Chez Thomas Amaulry, 1687. Engraving.

TX817 B64 S Printed Book and Periodical Collection, gift of the Friends of Winterthur

Nicholas de Blegny was a French entrepreneur who styled himself as "adviser and physician-artist to his Majesty the King." He specialized in the promotion and sale of supplies and equipment for making the newly introduced beverages of tea, coffee, and chocolate. Blegny's book extols the medicinal and social virtues of tea while providing recipes for its preparation and instructions for its serving and consumption. As one of the earliest books on tea, the volume contributed significantly to acceptance of the exotic beverage.

127.

Acknowledgments

Thanks are due those staff members who undertook the lion's share of work in producing this volume and the accompanying Grolier Club exhibition: Neville Thompson, exhibition curator, in company with Bert Denker, Richard McKinstry, Lois Price, and Jeanne Solensky. They were supported by the entire library staff: Claudia Ballou, Heather Clewell, Kathryn Coyle, Luz DeJesus, Laura Detrick, Pat Elliott, Laura Parrish, Katie Sikes, and Dot Wiggins. Recognition must also be given to the staff of Winterthur's Exhibitions Department, Registration Department, and Conservation Department as well as the staff and members of the Grolier Club, particularly Ed Lincoln. As always, I offer special thanks to the Publications Department, especially Onie Rollins, senior editor, and Susan Randolph, director. Finally, for her many years of support and leadership, my heartfelt gratitude to Winterthur Trustee Julia B. Leisenring, former chairman of the Academic Affairs Committee.

Gary Kulik
Deputy Director for Library, Collections
Management, and Academic Programs
Waldron Phoenix Belknap Librarian

Index

Within this index, the first number in page locators refers to the page; the number following the colon refers to specific catalogue entries on that page.